The Docent
Handbook 2
Revised Edition

Like the multi-colored pieces of glass in a kaleidoscope, docents from art museums, natural history and science museums, botanical gardens, children's museums and historical sites come together at the symposium to participate in a dialogue about the role and mission of docents.

Sponsored by the National Docent Symposium Council
www.nationaldocents.org

The Docent Handbook 2

ISBN: 978-0-692-03413-2

The kaleidoscope was designed by Jan Wallake, Toledo Art Museum, Toledo, Ohio.

For information about the National Docent Symposium Council and for ordering the *The Docent Handbook 2*, please visit www.nationaldocents.org.

Printed by Authority Publishing

The Docent Handbook was designed by Kate Ferrucci and Soontire Sutanont, Henry Radford Hope School of Fine Arts, Indiana University, Bloomington, Indiana

Contents

Acknowledgments

Twice in the history of the National Docent Symposium, docents have assumed the additional task of summarizing and publishing the material presented at the lectures and workshops during their symposia. The first such resource was published by the docents of the Oakland Museum of California in 1985, and the docents of the Denver Art Museum published the second in 1991. Over the years, thousands of copies of these handbooks have provided valuable ideas to many docents, guides and interpreters.

The National Docent Symposium Council, with the express permission of the two institutions, received right, title and interest in these resource books. Through a lengthy collaborative process, we combined, edited and added material to the original texts. We gratefully acknowledge the cooperation and support of the docents from the Oakland Museum of California and the Denver Art Museum. We also thank the Directors of the National Docent Symposium Council as well as docents and docent educators who inspired us and provided ideas for this project. We offer *The Docent Handbook* and hope that it will provide a stimulating resource for docents, guides and interpreters for many years to come.

Helga Keller, Docent
Indiana University Art Museum

Carole Kramer, Docent
Natural History Museum of Los Angeles County

The Docent Handbook was revised and augmented in 2016. Museums, the visitors coming to them and world around us have changed in important ways since the initial publication in 2001. We have kept intact the essential information and helpful suggestions from the original with profound appreciation for the wisdom and experience that it contains. We have added several new sections reflecting the increasingly diverse audiences for museums, the arrival of our digital world and evolving tour strategies geared to museums of all kinds. We have included web addresses for additional resources on given topics. We gratefully acknowledge contributions from members of the National Docent Symposium Council Directors and its Publications Committee and offer *The Docent Handbook 2*.

Betsy Vourlekis, Docent
National Docent Symposium Council Directors | Sackler Gallery of Art

Sybil Williamson, Docent
Hood Museum of Art at Dartmouth College

Introduction

The past few decades have seen a great increase in the number of new museums, the restoration and modernization of existing museums and new approaches to presenting objects. Museums preserve knowledge through the ages and have become essential elements of curricula in elementary and high schools as well as in universities.

Ever-increasing audiences of all ages are eager to experience museums and historical sites and to partake in enriching discovery tours and learning experiences.

In the museum environment, specially trained volunteers help the public to examine and appreciate art and artifacts, to explore the past through historical and ethnic treasures and to investigate our natural environment.

The knowledge base from which we learn is extremely broad, yet sometimes we overlook the basics. We are overwhelmed by numbers, speed and technology, and there seems little time for the muses. In view of the rapidly changing flow of information and development of new technologies, we should remember that humans are also deeply rooted in tradition, heritage and history—and therein lies our strength. It is this foundation on which docents can build knowledge that enables them to make a difference in today's world and to help others understand the world in which we live and dream.

Programs for the training of docents, guides and interpreters have existed for many decades. New approaches to leading tours and educating the public in museum settings are constantly being developed. The ideas and suggestions presented in this book have evolved out of hundreds of discussions, workshops and presentations led by docents, guides and interpreters.

In 1981 at the Indianapolis Art Museum, the concept of a National Docent Symposium as a forum for spirited discussions and the exchange of ideas was developed. Since then, bi-annual National Docent Symposia

have resulted in new insights into the art of presenting collections and exhibits to an ever-increasing number of people interested in exploring museums, historical sites and botanical gardens. It is in this spirit that we present ideas and suggestions about showing the collections of our institutions to the public.

The Term *Docent*

docent (do's'nt; G. do tsent') n. [G., earlier sp. of dozent, teacher, lecturer

< L. docens, prp. of docere, to teach]

1. In some American universities, a teacher or lecturer not on the regular faculty.

2. A tour guide and lecturer, as at a museum.

In this handbook the term *docent* describes docents, guides, interpreters and all those volunteers who:

- present to visitors, young and old, the beautiful and challenging collections in art museums,
- unlock the mysteries of earliest civilizations in archaeological museums,
- bring to life our heritage and history on historic sites and in historical museums,
- encourage young audiences to explore and discover, to think and to express themselves creatively in children's museums,
- lead us into the wondrous world of botanical gardens and nurture an understanding of nature and its delicate balance and
- bring us a feeling for the history, diversity, advances and challenges on our planet, for its peoples and its environments in science, technology, and natural history museums.

Each one of us is part of the larger community that makes up our institution. Most of us feel pride and a certain amount of ownership for our institution, and so we decided to incorporate into the Introduction a few ideas that are on our minds and certainly on the minds of many visitors.

Who Owns the Object? How Did It Get Here? What Is It Worth?

Museums collect objects because of their value, their uniqueness and rarity or because they were or are on the cutting edge of a major movement or new era. Museums play an important role in housing, protecting and preserving original art and artifacts.

Museums are interested in increasing audience involvement and participation with the goal of making visitors feel welcome and comfortable. Many visitors show increased interest in the history of the museum they visit, the provenance of the collections, how these collections were built or acquired and whether certain artifacts travel to special exhibits in other museums.

Where appropriate you can expand your tour and discussions into the following areas:

- the role of patrons and donors,
- the importance of gifts and acquisitions,
- the role of "Friends of Art (the Museum . . .)",
- ownership versus permanent loans,
- material of objects,
- provenance of objects,
- the condition of objects (Are they well preserved? Are they damaged? Do they show traces of repeated restoration work?),

- the place of the artist or sculptor and their work in the context of other works,
- number of available objects in a certain time period or category,
- the role of the museum in special exhibits (lending its collections to other museums or organizing its own special exhibits) and
- the role of museums as protectors and preservers.

Some museums hold collections in public trust. Be prepared to discuss the question of who owns the objects in such a museum:

- The institution?
- The board of trustees?
- The curators?
- The docents?
- The community at large?
- The museum visitor?

Visitors who feel invested in a museum and who will be allowed to take a glimpse behind the scenes might want to learn more about how the institution works; they might develop a sense of admiration, appreciation and support for the institution and the docent who leads them into a new experience.

1 Foundations

During the last two decades the educational role of the museum has gained importance as museums strive to expand visitor participation in a stimulating learning experience. A docent can expect to encounter both the inexperienced museum visitor and the sophisticated, well-traveled visitor who often expects a museum experience to surpass cultural television programs and Internet tours. Meeting school-based needs involves docents with students from preschool through high school. Therefore, the docent's challenge is to provide a comfortable, pleasant adventure for all through careful preparation and good speaking skills.

Treat Your Visitors as Your Personal Guests

Museum visitors appreciate helpfulness, respect, special attention, gracious manners and sensitive treatment. An effective docent quickly assesses the visitors' familiarity with the subject matter as well as their psychological and physical comfort so that a pleasant learning environment can be created.

Physical comfort involves clear orientation, instructive and legible signage, adequate lighting and comfortable seating. Did visitors arrive following a long trip? Is it necessary to check backpacks and coats? Are there special needs to be considered?

Psychological comfort involves your treatment of the visitor. Be sure to extend a warm welcome and offer help in finding various facilities. Share orientation material and explain floor plans. An engaging smile and informative directions can go a long way.

Intellectual comfort involves hearing and accepting visitors' ideas and concerns as valid. How can you make visitors feel comfortable at their present knowledge level? How can you make them feel confident in their ability to understand and appreciate what they will see and hear?

Visitors come to the museum to learn by seeing something they have never seen before, discovering details they might have missed during a previous visit or acquiring techniques that they can apply now and during future museum visits. They expect a pleasant social experience as well as a stimulating learning experience. Build on children's natural socializing to your advantage by using paired activities. Point out historical connections by making contrasts and comparisons. Visitors enjoy sharing discoveries with partners. Whenever possible, use touchable materials to lead them into questioning.

People come to a museum to have a good time and to participate through conversation. The more control you give the group, the more powerful and confident they will feel, therefore encouraging them to participate. Your tours will pay dividends if you teach them skills that they can apply after their visit as well.

Who's in Charge?

If you want to teach visitors new skills, it is essential that you give them opportunities to practice what they have learned. If you want to teach your audience how to read a work of art or diorama, lead them into a discovery experience by stimulating their eyes and minds. Allow them to respond to you and to communicate their observations.

In order to let your visitors play a more active role, you need to give up some of the authority you had previously enjoyed when using the lecture method, even though you might be concerned about the progress of a tour when you step out of the leadership role into a participatory role. You also might be wondering why you should prepare a detailed tour—after all, your tour contains your personal ideas and expressions about the objects you plan to show. This is understandable, since letting visitors' interests and responses shape your tour is much less predictable than following a pre-planned agenda or script. You will discover that empowering your audience will open up an entirely new museum experience for you and for your tour participants.

Visitors want a personally relevant experience. In natural history museums, ask visitors to compare their own geographical or cultural areas to what they see in the exhibit. In art museums, a painting can transport the visitor to another time and place, reveal the artist's mind and create a human connection with an inanimate object. You can try to draw out relevant experiences by creating an environment conducive to sharing personal associations and observations free of value judgments.

If discussing 18th-century decorative arts, for example, you may want to ask:

- *Which pieces of furniture look valuable and why?*
- *Which objects do you think took a lot of time to create and why?*

In a historic house, a possible theme may be: "All people need food, clothing and shelter." Your questions might be:

- *How did people prepare and store their food?*
- *How did they stay warm in winter?*
- *What materials did they use for clothing?*

When talking about landscape painting in an art museum you could ask:

- *Would you like to visit this place? Why?*
- *How does this painting make you feel?*
- *What did the artist do to achieve a certain effect?*

Know Your Subject

An understanding of broad concepts as well as specific information about objects is essential. Acquire an overview of cultural and social history, art history, natural history, history, science, archaeology, anthropology and botany, reflecting the subjects on which your institution focuses. Become familiar with the content of special exhibits. Use quotes, anecdotes and stories to enliven your presentation.

Know Your Audience

The more you know about your audience, the better you are able to match the tour to their interests, needs and abilities. Check the language skills and special needs, if necessary. Study learning theories, communication skills and group characteristics and apply this knowledge to your museum tour.

While preparing for a school tour, you might want to call the teacher and find out what the class is studying. Look at the curriculum materials and, if possible, visit the classroom.

Select a Theme

Choose a theme and a few ideas you want to emphasize. The more focused you are, the better your chances are that your group will remember relevant facts. Your theme should be age appropriate and pertain to the gallery objects. State your theme clearly and repeat it throughout the tour:

Art:	• Geometric shapes in art and architecture
	• How artists see the human face
	• The role of gods and heroes in various cultures around the world
History:	• Life at home in the past century
	• The role of women in society then & now
Science:	• What is a mammal/dinosaur/bird?
	• Adaptation to the environment
	• Minerals & their uses, past and present

Establish Your Goals and Objectives

A well-organized tour has clear goals and objectives. Think about what you want your visitors to learn and remember. If your goal is that at the end of the tour your visitors will be able to identify differences between species, name parts of a plant or describe elements of a painting, prepare your questions accordingly. Know what you want to accomplish.

Plan Your Tour

Plan your tour by writing an outline for your theme, goals and objectives as well as the introduction, content and conclusion. Prepare a list that highlights the objects you plan to cover and the activities, questions and transitions that reinforce your theme. Develop a pattern. Avoid reading or memorizing the tour script, or presenting it verbatim.

Does the information you have about the group allow you to anticipate what the group might want to see or how they might react to your questions? What learning styles and skills might your visitors prefer?

Be Flexible

Sometimes visitors become interested in an object in the gallery that might not be included in your tour plans. Therefore, be familiar with all objects and their locations in the gallery that you plan to visit.

Check the route for your tour, making sure that the objects you want to highlight are on display. Practice a variety of presentation styles, use different vocabulary and plan different starting points and various time allotments.

On the Tour

Think about your position in relation to your group and the object. Make sure that they can see what you are describing and that you do not block the visitors' view. Before encouraging someone else to look at an object, see it yourself. Sit on the floor and notice what is easy or difficult to see. Be aware of how the light hits the painting or artifact from various positions. Take into consideration that viewing a three-dimensional object is more complex in terms of visitors' moves than viewing a two-dimensional object.

Use appropriate and objective vocabulary. Be careful not to impart a particular point of view by your choice of words. Use your voice effectively; vary the tone and pace of delivery.

Maintaining eye contact is one of the most important factors in establishing a good rapport with all your tour participants.

YOUR PERSONAL NOTES

Use gestures in a restrained, natural manner when speaking and watch your non-verbal cues to ensure that you are holding the group's attention.

There is no single right way to look at art and nature. Allow visitors to respond to your explanations and to express their own observations.

Enjoy Yourself

Thoughtfulness and politeness are important qualities of a docent. Smiles, humor, shared laughter and steady eye contact are essential. Enthusiasm is contagious.

If you enjoy what you are doing and if you are excited about your subject, your museum and your group, your visitors will know it **and you will be off to a successful tour!**

2 Points of Departure

Establishing rapport and knowing your audience are the keys to a successful tour. As you greet the group, introduce yourself, get acquainted with your audience and ask them about their expectations. Share some of your own experiences and observations.

Introduction
Introduce your institution, explain its history and its mission. Highlight the special collections or exhibits. You might want to explain some of the museum's activities and describe the functions it serves within the community.

Tell Your Visitors Something about Yourself
Introduce yourself! Share some of your interests with your visitors. Explain the meaning of docent, being careful not to describe yourself as an expert but rather as a volunteer who will support them in developing museum discovery skills. Emphasize that you serve as a connector between visitors and the objects and that you will embark on a shared learning experience. Present a brief overview of the planned tour. The amount of time you spend with each object sends a message about how long they should explore that object.

Find Out Something about Your Visitors
Have they ever visited this museum? If the answer is yes, ask what they remember best about the previous visit. If no, what do they expect to learn on your tour? Consider visitors' prior knowledge and attitudes. The insight into visitors' backgrounds will help you structure your tour.

If your tour participants are school children, ask them what they expect to see or whether they need to fulfill certain requirements. You might want to ask students what they are studying in school. Is this visit an introduction to the subject matter or does it serve as reinforcement to a course curriculum? Would they like to explore specific topics or themes? Do they have specific questions?

Let Your Visitors Know Your Plan
Briefly discuss the theme for your tour. Tell visitors what they can expect to see and the approximate time it will take to complete the tour. Explore what connections to everyday life can be made from the content of the tour. Present the coming attractions that will stimulate interest and make them comfortable, but do not spend a lot of time telling visitors what you plan to show them.

What You Do Is as Important as What You Say
Visitors will look upon you as the leader. You should be poised and self-confident, using excellent speaking skills and grammar. Be aware of your body language, your facial expressions and the messages you send to your audience. A glance, nod, gesture, smile or frown can communicate and control without interrupting the flow of learning. How you look expresses how you feel about yourself and about the museum you represent.

The following questions may raise awareness about your touring style:

- *How many times do I look at an object while I discuss it?*
- *How much eye contact do I maintain with the audience?*
- *How much of the information I share is based on my insights, and how much is derived from the object?*
- *How many and what kinds of comparisons do I make?*
- *How often do I shift focus to help visitors see different aspects of the painting, artifact, or diorama?*

The No-Touch Rule
There are many good ways to remind tour participants to refrain from touching objects while touring the collections:

- *Draw on their experience—have they seen objects that are badly worn from too many fingerprints (e.g., shiny parts on brass and bronze sculptures, greasy stains on stone surfaces, fingerprints and scuff marks on walls)?*

- *Show them the impact of fingerprints on a surface—pass around a pair of glasses, a mirror or a piece of metal*
- *Refer to their senses—ask the group to explore traces of perspiration, salt and oil on their skin.*
- *Remind them that glass cases might be fragile and unable to withstand the pressure of people leaning against them.*

What to Do if Your Young Visitors Enter the Museum with Excess Energy

You may want to suggest some relaxation exercises or a stretch-and-wiggle game to your younger audience before you embark on the tour. Ask your group to stand on their tiptoes with the hands extended and to freeze in that position. Then let them "shake out all the wiggles." When they stretch as high as they can, ask them to imagine a painting or an animal that is three times as tall.

Relaxation Methods for the Mature Audience

For your mature audience, you might find some humorous anecdotes or stories to share. Laughing together relaxes the public and breaks the ice.

The best way to help a group relax and focus is to set an example. Close your eyes as you begin to speak to them, take a deep relaxing breath, exhale naturally and speak slowly in a modulated voice. Ask them to imagine being in a peaceful spot where they are completely at ease. Follow this breathing exercise with a visualization technique.

In art museums, the docent can describe walking through a door painted in their favorite color. As they walk through, they could feel that color washing over them, bathing them in relaxation and, when they were ready, they could open their eyes and come back to the room.

The same technique can be used in a natural history museum to help visitors enter a diorama. Ask them to close their eyes and imagine a plane ride to Africa, feeling the hot air hitting their faces as they exit the plane and then open their eyes to see animals gathered at a watering hole.

To Hold Your Visitors' Attention

Engage your audience. Asking questions allows you to gain useful information and set the tone for the

tour. Your questions will indicate that you value visitors' responses and that you are interested in meeting their expectations. Allow young visitors to act as leaders, to model appropriate behavior and to participate in role-playing without displaying any favoritism. Shower students with positive attention. Show interest in your visitors' experience, engage them in discussions, respond to their remarks and, if necessary, lead them gently back to the goals of the tour. A good portion of humor, praise, encouragement and enthusiasm will win over even the toughest audiences.

Ask yourself the following questions:

- *Have I selected appropriate activities for my visitors' age group?*
- *Have I actively involved the students?*
- *Does my pace and variety keep their interest?*
- *Can they see and hear?*
- *Am I weaving the various elements of my theme together in my questions and transitions?*

In Making Transitions

A successful transition provides continuity because it builds on the discoveries and observations from one gallery to the next. Transitions also provide a sense of excitement and anticipation during the tour. It can take the form of a game or an activity to reinforce a theme, but words are useful too.

Here are some examples:

- *Let's see "how people kept warm" again in the next room.*
- *What is changing in the environment as we move to the next diorama?*
- *We have just learned how baskets were used in the last century. When we visit the next gallery, let's look for additional uses.*
- *As we leave this gallery and enter the next gallery, let's see what invention (or historical/social/religious event) challenged artists to explore new styles.*
- *Let's see how the people and their societies used materials (clay, wood) to create objects when we explore the next exhibit.*

How to Finish a Tour

It is tempting to tack on more facts and objects once you realize that the end of the touring time is approaching. From the visitor's point of view, though, the last precious moments are better spent reiterating the theme and recapping the main points of the tour. Invite visitors to describe the most surprising information they learned about an object. Encourage children to think about the importance of a specific object, what they remember best and what they liked or disliked on the tour. Since it is not possible to see it all in one hour, invite visitors to return with their families and explore other galleries or exhibits in your museum.

Looking Back on Your Tour
With each tour you conduct you'll gain new insights and different perspectives. It is beneficial that you

reflect on the experience and consider the following questions:

- *What did I try to accomplish?*
- *Did I succeed in meeting my objectives?*
- *Did I use appropriated vocabulary?*
- *How did my tour participants react?*
- *Why did a particular activity work well?*
- *Was the timing right?*
- *What could have worked better?*

YOUR PERSONAL NOTES

3 On Language, or: What's in a Word?

Language does more than transmit information. It is a most powerful means of communicating attitudes and values, so it must be used thoughtfully. Sometimes the words you use do not send the message you intended. It is difficult to think through the implications of each of your words while you are giving a tour, and it is equally hard to remember exactly what was said afterward, so it is important to reflect on the vocabulary you plan to use before you meet your visitors.

Your Audience

The words you use to talk *about* your audience are just as important as those you use when speaking *to* them. Begin by considering the meaning of some words that can challenge assumptions about the docent's role. In a subtle but profound way, the words chosen to describe the audience influence the way they are treated.

Starting with the word *audience*, ask yourself:

- *What kind of relationship do I have with an audience?*
- *What are the best ways of reaching an audience?*
- *Does an audience usually take an active or a passive role?*
- *How do I behave as a member of an audience?*
- *How do I like to behave in a museum?*

You can also describe the people you serve as *visitors*, so reflect for a moment about the following questions:

- *What kind of relationship do I have with the visitor?*
- *How do I accommodate a visitor?*
- *How do I speak to a visitor?*
- *How do I expect a visitor to respond?*
- *How do I behave as a visitor?*

You may take another step and replace the words *audience* and *visitor* with *guest*:

- *What kind of relationship do I have with a guest?*
- *How do I welcome a guest?*
- *How do I converse with a guest?*
- *How do I expect a guest to respond?*
- *How do I behave as a guest?*

Finally, use the metaphor *consumer* and consider the following questions:

- *How do consumers expect to be treated?*
- *Could my tour compete with other leisure time activities?*
- *Are my tours worth paying for, in the sense of supporting my museum?*

Language offers many ways of communicating and often the most expedient route is chosen. But this may not be the best way to address the visitor. Although convenient, terms like *Native American, Hispanic* or *Latino* may not be comfortable to your audience. It is important to be sensitive to what is accepted in your community, because more than vocabulary is at stake. It is a matter of identity. In these days of challenging accepted definitions, the best way to be sure you are using a term that is acceptable to your audience is to ask them honestly and openly. Visitors are delighted to assist the docent because they appreciate the museum's sensitivity to their language. Such effort will pay big dividends in the development of new audiences.

Your Role as a Docent

The words you use to describe yourself shape your role and the way you perform. Consider the word *docent*. To you, its meaning is clear and specific, but most people would have to find its meaning in a dictionary. If you look it up, you will find it defined as "teacher, lecturer." Is this how you want people to view you? Both *teacher* and *lecturer* have authoritarian connotations that visitors may find intimidating. Perhaps you should ask yourself, "What kind of rapport do I establish with my guests by introducing myself with a Latin word that is not part of their vocabulary?" If you want to use the word *docent*, think about enriching the definition by adding phrases such as: "A docent is like *a spark, an interpreter, a guide or a link between curators and visitors.*"

The Collections in Your Institution

Vocabulary is very important in describing the objects in your collections, because the wider the vocabulary, the sharper the perception. Whether you talk about *baboons* or *Botticellis*, you must be able to articulate what you see. The more you see, the more you must expand your vocabulary to describe your observations. The words you use are like symbols that represent the objects you present. Give visitors the opportunity to talk, to think out loud and to verbally explore. This experience will create a deep excitement about the subject matter that in turn might bring to the surface a multitude of attitudes and meanings and memories of past experiences. Visitors will sharpen their perceptions and be motivated to observe.

By using evocative language, you can bring objects to life. You can guide your visitors' eyes and minds and inspire and excite them. Docents can use verbal language to translate visual language. Employing adjectives, adverbs, alliteration and onomatopoeia to describe paintings, dioramas or historic settings greatly enriches visitors' experiences. Evocative language can actually help visitors to understand and experience what may be a very different world for them.

Appeal to the senses by using words that encourage visitors to see, smell and hear:

- *A landscape can be serene, peaceful, lonely, quiet, busy, sunny, sublime.*
- *Some figures in the family portrait appear to be richly dressed, puzzled, frightened, relaxed, secretive, intimidating.*

Describing paintings, you may state:

- *The potato eaters gather wearily around the table.*
- *The hunters energetically chase the stag.*
- *The mountains majestically tower over the tiny hamlet.*

Using alliteration, you may lead your visitors into discovering exhibits from an entirely different perspective:

- *The wolves are howling in the icy winter wind.*
- *The charging buffaloes create a lot of noise as they thunder across the placid plains.*
- *A relaxed couple stands near the wind-whipped water, watching flags flapping in the breeze.*

Senses challenge visitors:

- *to feel the heat, to see the water moving, to hear the crowd cheering*
- *to smell the culinary, mythical and medicinal powers of scent*
- *to hear birds chirping, whales singing, church bells ringing and leaves rustling in the wind*

Senses invite visitors to experience various fragrances:

- *Pick a mint leaf to crush and enjoy its delicious aroma.*
- *Pluck and crumble a basil leaf in order to compare its aroma to that of a pinched thyme leaf.*

Explore how artists attempted to translate musical structures, compositional laws, rhythmic movement and sound patterns into visual language. Looking at an abstract painting, you may ask visitors:

- *Do you hear anything? Chords? Dissonant or harmonic chords? Flat sounds? Soothing, comforting sounds?*
- *Can you associate certain colors with certain tones or even certain instruments?*
- *Which musical properties did the artist express?*

Be careful about using technical terms to describe your collections. Correct terminology plays a vital role in accurate scholarship, but it must be chosen wisely in docent tours. Never use a word to impress someone with your knowledge. The best way to communicate is in the clearest, simplest and most appropriate terms possible. If you must employ technical or scientific terms, make sure that visitors comprehend your presentation. It is far better to err on the side of clarity and define any term that may be unfamiliar to any member of your audience.

The Museum Experience

Everyone brings their individual life experiences and associations to their museum visit. Thinking in an audience-centered fashion allows you to tap into visitors' own observations, connections and reactions to what they are seeing. Often this makes what the museum offers personally meaningful and more memorable than only providing information, interesting as the information may be.

Rather than presenting expert opinions or your own interpretation of objects, share your feelings, insights and thoughts with your group and ask for theirs. By using a discussion model instead of a lecture, you engage visitors in conversation and create opportunities for them to offer differing points of view. Museum tours then become more participatory and stimulating.

Entertainment is another concept that should influence your tours. This does not imply a compromise of academic standards. But docents should face the fact that if they are not enlightening and entertaining, they will lose their audiences.

Consider your tour content as a tool that is a means to an end, not an end in itself. Alternatively, think of tours as building blocks that can be used to create something larger. Comments can be viewed as puzzle pieces necessary to the solution of a problem. Adopting these practical attitudes helps you encourage visitors to use the information you present. Visitors can pull the information apart and put it back together to discover new patterns and create new meanings. Developing these skills can transform museum visitors into museum users.

Thinking about Cultural Heritage and *Labels*

It is important to be sensitive to issues of cultural identity and values in your community. Cultural identity can be defined by religion, race, nationality, geography, or ethnic background or any combination of these. At times visitors' self-defined cultural heritage may influence how they view and understand what the museum is presenting and may differ from what you may have been taught by curators and scholars. Respecting differing views while still presenting the museum's information requires acceptance of the validity of the visitor's personal "truth" in this setting.

Although terms like *Native American, Hispanic, Latino* or *Minority* seem convenient, they might not be comfortable and acceptable terms for members of your audience and risk stereotyping individuals. The best way to avoid alienating children and adults is to develop an understanding of the complexities of growing up or living with two or more languages in an environment culturally different from your own. Open-mindedness and sensitivity can allow for a valuable learning experience for all.

Equally important are the words used to describe different age levels. A good general rule is: "If you can avoid labels when referring to people, do so." It is always better to describe people as individuals rather than categories. When you must generalize about a group, you can still acknowledge the individuality of each member of your group by focusing on what you have in common rather than what separates you. Older people and older adults suggest qualities you share as human beings, whereas the elderly and the aged suggest differences. Older adult may be preferable to senior citizen or mature adult, because these terms suggest their opposites—junior citizen and immature adult. Sometimes you may feel that you just can't win in your efforts to find the right word. It's okay to make mistakes. Keep an open mind, try to stay aware of preferred usage, and above all, be personable.

The Linguistically Diverse Audience

Be prepared to meet groups that pose linguistic challenges. Not only foreign tourists, but also more and more groups with limited English proficiency visit your institution and participate in tours. The number of non-English-speaking children has increased and bilingual education is a fact in many schools.

Here are some helpful suggestions:

- *Add a few sessions on pronunciation to docent training programs in areas with large Spanish-speaking populations.*
- *Greet your guests in various languages to be determined by the visitors' backgrounds.*
- *Avoid a xenophobic tone when presenting exhibits.*
- *Build connections between your collections and the cultures of your visitors.*
- *Give visitors the opportunity to assist you with difficult terms in their native tongue. Welcome their participation in explaining certain objects and social or historic facts.*
- *Keep your language simple and clearly understandable; avoid baby talk or endearments.*
- *Use visuals and appropriate, non-offensive gestures.*
- *Allow plenty of time after asking questions so that your visitors have time to reflect and are able to formulate their responses.*

4 Learning Styles

Museum settings present a multitude of possibilities to accommodate various learning styles because they provide a forum for discussions and discoveries. Ethnic museums celebrate the fact that people in other places have lifestyles and habitats that are different from our own. History museums afford a journey into the past and allow comparisons to the present. Objects in art museums provide an opportunity to explore the creative processes and show examples of aesthetic and pragmatic solutions. Science museums give us the opportunity to explore the difference between what we see on the surface of objects and what we know about their inner workings.

Thinking about Thinking and Learning

Docents must become familiar with learning styles when planning and conducting tours. Visitors are challenged to think about the objects and exhibits they see and to learn about their uses and meanings.

Many theories about cognitive processes have evolved over the past few decades. As an example, the four types of thinkers defined by J. P. Guilford (1967) and E. P. Torrance (1967) are described here:

Fluid thinkers generate a large quantity of ideas, options and possibilities. Encourage them with questions like: "How many different reasons can you think of for . . . ?"

Flexible thinkers can shift their mental perspective or see one thing in a variety of manifestations. Pose questions like: "How else might you choose to . . . ?"

Original thinkers can develop highly personalized responses that reflect a unique perspective. Ask original thinkers questions like: "If you were going to give this work a title, what would you call it?"

Elaborative thinkers can embellish thoughts with exceptional richness of details or texture. Use questions like: "How would you describe the texture/sound/taste of . . . ?"

Everyone learns in a different way. By exploring diverse learning styles, you can gain a better understanding of how you learn and can discover how other people learn. Your ultimate goal is to reach the broadest possible spectrum of your audience. Because everyone coming to the museum brings with them learned attitudes, feelings and previous experiences that differ from each other, it is important to put what you have to say into as many forms of communication as possible. You can reach the largest audience if you communicate in visual, verbal and physical terms. Docents should acknowledge and value different learning styles among visitors, because they enrich and enliven tours.

If everyone learned in a systematic way, we would all start with concrete experiences, using our senses to gather as much information as possible. Then we would move on to reflective observation, collecting more data as we began to formulate a plan. From there we would move into the realm of abstract conceptualization, thinking about the best way of putting our plan into action. We would complete the cycle through active experimentation, evaluating what we had done. However, people are not machines that can be programmed; therefore, most of us do not learn this way. Some of us will not act until we get lots of information, while others act first and get information later.

During previous Symposia, experts like Rhonda Wilkerson (Excel), Bernice McCarthy (4MAT System) and David Kolb (Learning Style Inventory) presented ideas that describe four approaches to shaping the way we learn. They suggest various characteristics for each type of learner.

Type 1 learners rely on their senses and feelings. They contribute to a tour because they enjoy brainstorming. They integrate experiences into their lives; therefore, they are likely to consider the information you present from the standpoint of what it means to them personally. On a museum tour, they want to establish a rapport with the docent. They appreciate a friendly, caring approach.

Positive attributes: cooperative, friendly, thoughtful, supportive, good team player or committee member.

Negative attributes: softhearted, slow to act, values harmony over growth, lacks initiative.

Type 1 learners approach an object and ask, "Why?" You can encourage imaginative thinking by asking questions that help this visitor make personal connections with objects.

Type 2 learners gather information and then reflect on it. They combine what they see with what they know. They want all the facts and prefer to get them in a logical sequence. They look to the docent for information. The docent wins their respect by being knowledgeable.

Positive attributes: logical, accurate, dependable, conservative.

Negative attributes: indecisive, unwilling to take risks, impersonal nature, avoids involvement.

Type 2 learners ask, "What?" Foster analytical thinking by asking questions that elicit information from the visitor. This often provides an opening for you to present information.

Type 3 learners also start with information, but they are eager to act on it. These visitors take an active approach to learning; therefore, they benefit from hands-on experience. They work hard to develop their skills; they test theories and solve problems pragmatically. They would rather figure something out for themselves than be given the answer. They want the docent to ask questions that will lead them toward discovering something on their own.

Positive attributes: efficient, task oriented, independent, decisive, opinionated.

Negative attributes: acts hastily, impatient, bossy, critical.

Type 3 learners ask, "How?" You can build on their common sense by asking questions that explore their abilities to apply information.

Type 4 learners act on their senses and feelings and want to teach themselves, so they may not want to join a docent-led tour. If they do, they enjoy a docent who asks questions that they would raise themselves. Wherever they go, they are on a journey of self-discovery; their museum experience will be no exception to the rule. They will make an enthusiastic addition to any tour.

Positive attributes: stimulating, thought provoking, outgoing, enthusiastic.

Negative attributes: impulsive, lacks follow-through, avoids isolation.

Type 4 learners ask, "What if . . . ?" Stimulate dynamic thinking by asking questions that suggest ways to expand upon the information you present.

Developing Questions for Different Types of Learners

The following description of the 17th-century Dutch painting from c. 1629, *Young Man Having a Tooth Extracted* by Jan Miense Molenaer (c. 1610–1668), serves as an example to illustrate how to develop questions that reflect the various types of learners:

> Light and dark dramatize the subject matter in this Baroque painting. Three non-idealized human figures are the central focus: A distraught young man dressed in a robe is seated on a chair, his mouth wide open. He leans against a table, the right arm extended, his hand clutching a jug on the table. A man dressed in a fancy coat eagerly leans toward the young man. Using both hands he pulls down the young man's chin in order to examine the wide-open mouth. A smiling young woman stands behind the dentist, facing the patient, her left hand raised in a waving gesture. The three figures are highlighted by an invisible source of light, while the rest of the room is bathed in darkness, but for a rhomboid-shaped window on the left side of the painting and a rectangular-shaped open door leading into another part of the house in the right-hand side of the painting.

The painting is exhibited in the North Carolina Art Museum.

Type 1

- *Why do you think the girl smiling and gesturing?*
- *Why do you think the artist choose this subject?*
- *Why do you think there aren't any details in the setting?*
- *Why do you think the dentist is wearing such fancy clothes?*

Type 2

- *What does the man have in his mouth?*
- *What shapes can you find in the painting?*
- *What's the difference between this dental office and a modern dentist's office?*
- *What direction is the light coming from?*

Type 3

- *How will the dentist pull the tooth?*
- *How does he get the patient to sit still?*
- *How do you think the patient feels?*
- *How can the dentist see in the dim light?*

Type 4

- *What if you were the one sitting in that chair?*
- *What if the dentist pulled the wrong tooth?*
- *What if the action took place in another century?*
- *What if the painting were done by Picasso?*

Any tour group may include all four types of learners. Therefore, when you plan a tour, develop a series of questions and answers tailored to each learning style.

YOUR PERSONAL NOTES

5 Know Your Audience

School-Aged Visitors

Schools, museums and docents are concerned with developing effective methods to introduce young audiences to a valuable museum experience. In-school visits, slide and video presentations, learning centers, hands-on corners, art carts, library resources, pamphlets and the Internet are designed to prepare successful museum visits for young people that will hopefully lay the foundation for a lifelong interest in museum going.

Visits to museums, historical homes and gardens mean a significant change in the daily schedule of young people; they are required to slow down, to concentrate, to carefully observe and reflect. Children, young students and adults learn from an infinite variety of sources. Your challenge is to incorporate these sources of imagination and creativity into your tours. Your tour is supposed to lead to questions that provoke curiosity, exploration and discussion. Young visitors enjoy fantasy play, role-play, investigations, purposeful looking, and interaction with objects.

When working with school groups, the docent needs to know what the students are familiar with and what they are looking for. A school and grade's curriculum goals are increasingly important; teachers frequently can only justify museum visits if specific goals can be addressed. Whenever possible, the docent should call or e-mail the teacher several days before a scheduled tour and ask:

- *How have you prepared the students for this tour? What do they already know about what they will be seeing?*
- *Have you talked about the specific objects they will see?*
- *Have you told the students to look for specific information? Will they be taking notes, taking pictures, or filling in work sheets?*

- *Do you have any suggestions for making this group attentive or responsive? Are there any special learning or physical needs we should be aware of?*
- *Have you discussed museum etiquette with the students?*
- *What are you goals for the visit?*

Children in particular may have to become familiar with the gallery before they are able to embark on learning activities. Assess special comfort needs:

- *How will they feel about an imposing museum building?*
- *Will a large room, visitor traffic flow, noise or different levels of lighting affect their ability to concentrate?*
- *Are exits, restrooms and water fountains clearly marked?*
- *Do they feel uncomfortable facing a wall while there is a lot of activity going on in another part of the gallery?*
- *Are students who have special needs participating?*

Keeping in mind that there are vast developmental differences for each age category, consider the following ideas:

Kindergarten, Grades 1–2 (ages 5 to 7)

Tours should be kept short, no longer than 30 to 45 minutes. Limit the number of objects—less is more—and encourage children to choose some of the objects. Whenever possible, sit down with children in front of an artwork, artifact or diorama and help them focus their attention. Children in this age category are ready for an open-ended challenge that provides opportunities for observation and comparisons among objects.

Look for a theme from object to object and over time:

- *We'll see families in different countries and eras.*
- *Let's try to imagine what the characters in the paintings are thinking.*

Explore the elements of art and introduce a basic art vocabulary:

- *We are going to look at colors.*
- *We are going to look at shapes.*

Explore the definition of habitat in history or science dioramas:

- *Tell us about your neighborhood, your home or your room.*
- *Tell us about the habitat we see before us.*

Focus on detail:

- *We are going to try to find a black dog in each painting.*
- *We are going to try to find a meat eater in each diorama.*

Children translate a picture into a simpler language of pictorial symbols. You can gain a lot of insight into the child's mind by presenting a drawing activity and comparing the results with the original artwork.

- *Try doing a body sculpture or a movement activity by asking children to mimic the actions in sculptures or dioramas.*
- *Let children tell a story about what they are seeing and what in the work makes them see it that way.*
- *Touch and describe the skin textures of mammals, birds and reptiles.*
- *Develop map skills by using maps with brightly colored continents, countries and oceans.*

Grades 3–6 (ages 8 to 11)

Children are eager to explore, discover and learn. They are interested in why and how things were made, how long it took to make them and what they were used for.

They enjoy participating in discussion and observing similarities and differences among objects. Children begin to step out of the imaginary world and develop a greater awareness of facts and reality.

Examine how art and artifacts reflect other times, people and places.

Examine the materials, tools and techniques that artists use in creating paintings, prints, ceramics and sculptures.

Explore the history of the Earth with the use of a globe to introduce plate tectonics. Compare different rock formations by letting them hold and feel samples of rocks.

Explore the physics of light and color using mirrors and prisms.

Explore various cultures and people with different heritages by comparing and contrasting styles in clothing, houses and tools.

Introduce the concept of a time line with the following activities:

- *Use a long string with a knot at the end, representing human evolution.*
- *Visualize a skyscraper with a coin placed on top.*
- *Think about "2 seconds before 12 o'clock."*
- *Assign a certain number of years to each step in the staircase of your museum and have visitors mark events that occurred ten, fifty and one hundred or more years ago.*

Early Years of Adolescence—Middle School Years (ages 12 to 14)

Adolescents enjoy fun and laughter and a sense of independence. Socializing is of great importance. The museum tour is looked upon as freedom from the classroom. They enjoy discussions among themselves, holding hands and leaning on each other. A tour of adolescents can very quickly become fragmented. Allowing individual or pairs choice with "report back" to the whole group can be effective. Gallery activities promote group togetherness as well.

Students in this age group want to know what they are supposed to learn on the tour and what should be accomplished; they want a meaningful experience. You can contribute to a successful tour by setting rules for the tour and for the discussion. Provide guidance and leadership. A well-prepared tour with focus on discovery and inquiry is essential. The following suggestions may be a good starting point:

- *How would you describe this work to a visitor who has never been to a museum?*
- *Try to describe this painting or diorama to a blind friend.*
- *Compare family life of the past, as illustrated in the paintings, rooms or dioramas, to present-day customs.*

The World of Teenagers—High School Years

Teenagers are a terrific museum audience—if you are prepared to accept them as equal partners in your tour and discussions. Ideally, groups should be no larger than 10 to 12 students per docent. Small groups will allow you to present information in ways that will reach everyone.

Approach them as adults, treat them with respect—and accept that they will act like children at any given moment. Teenagers can sound rude, expressing themselves in their own language, and yet they are eager to connect and embrace new ideas and experiences.

At the beginning of the tour, ask teenagers what they are interested in seeing and discussing, and what they want to accomplish during the tour. Give teenagers the opportunity to demonstrate and discuss their interests, knowledge and understanding of the subject matter. Take into consideration what they already know and let them select some of the objects for discussion. Allow them to establish their own identity; allow them to choose their partners for group activities. Pose questions such as:

* *What is in a museum?*
* *What happens in a museum?*
* *What inspires people to visit museums?*
* *Tell me something about this object that is interesting or disturbing to you.*

Shift focus back and forth between your goals for the tour and their insights and ideas by developing creative questioning. Value their opinions and insights. Draw upon all their senses and link information to many different subject areas and personal experiences. Try to relate the subject or information to their lives and ask for their opinions and interpretation. Let them know that you are learning from each other while touring the exhibits together. Their suggestions might give you additional ideas for your tour.

Focus on questions that require decision making and explore the reasoning behind the decisions:

* *If you could choose one of the artworks you have seen, which would you choose and why would you choose it?*
* *What environmental concerns do we face today?*
* *How do you feel about exotic plants imported into our country and planted among our native plants?*
* *Can you name such a plant and describe its impact on the local environment?*

Choose specific questions that are of interest to teenagers. Try asking questions that evoke feelings:

* *What do you feel this artist is expressing in this landscape?*
* *How might it have felt to be a "knight in shining armor" riding off into a battle?*
* *Why do "ready-mades" qualify as artwork?*

Ask questions with focus on the exploration of styles and subjects:

* *How does the interior of a 19th-century home differ from that of a modern home?*
* *What are the similarities and differences when we compare the artifacts of the Northwest Coast Indians to those of the Indians of the Southwest?*

Lead them into recognizing changes in one artist's work or materials throughout the years:

* *Was the artist exploring a new direction in art?*
* *In which way did the artist use materials to create the work?*

Explore differences and similarities:

* *What characteristics do these plants share?*
* *How are they different?*
* *In what ways are the customs of this culture similar to or different from our own?*

You can use "tasks" to challenge students and to allow them choice and control. Discussing together about their choices promotes participation and insight.

* *Find the object that intrigues you as to how it was used or how it was made.*
* *Choose the two paintings that present the greatest contrast in mood for you.*
* *Choose an object that makes you curious about the culture that produced it.*

Some things to avoid: Remember not to lecture, ramble, over-explain or present too many facts or too much information. Don't spend too much time on one object. Don't talk down to young people, and don't be condescending. Become your group's teacher's best friend. After all, teachers entrust you with a group of children whom they know best. Teachers are as interested in a valuable museum experience as you are.

A good combination of humor and laughter, clear, sophisticated language and a relaxed, friendly attitude will narrow the gap between you and your young audience and assure a rewarding experience. [See for example "Raising Docent Confidence in Engaging Students on School Tours" in *Journal of Museum Education,* vol. 8, no. 3, 2013]

Multi-Age or Home School Groups

Home schooling is a growing modality. Often children of several families may participate together. Some private schools do not teach strictly by grade and age level and may bring a multi-aged group for a visit. It is important to establish a courteous relationship with visitors, no matter how challenging it might be to meet the demands and interests of a variety of aged children. Keep in mind that adults in charge of the schooling have goals and objectives for learning that can be tied to the museum visit. To assure a valuable museum experience for all tour participants, consider the following suggestions:

Tour Preparation

Ideally, the scheduling coordinator in your institution will request the following information from small private schools and home schooled groups:

- *day and time of the tour,*
- *list of objects,*
- *desired learning experience (fulfillment of a curriculum, highlight tour, thematic tour),*
- *ages of tour participants,*
- *number of teachers and chaperones accompanying the group and special needs that should be met; e.g., whether it will be necessary to accommodate babies, toddlers and strollers.*

This information is necessary in order to organize a stimulating tour that meets the expectations and learning goals for each participant in the group. Pre-tour packets of information should be sent to the coordinator or the contact person of the group with the suggestion that this information be distributed to all families involved.

Upon Arrival of the Group

Quickly assess the situation if you have no prior information:

- *What is the age range?*
- *How many teachers and chaperones are accompanying the group?*
- *Do some participants seem to be uncertain and not quite comfortable?*
- *How many babies and toddlers are accompanying the group?*

Introduce your museum and point out that you and your fellow docents have worked out tour topics that will meet the specific interests and expectations of the group. Explain touring styles and objectives for the tour and that you would like to fully focus on the children's interests.

Explain museum rules. In order to protect the objects on display and accommodate other visitors, museum rules must be observed. Ask for your group's support in keeping the collections safe and ensuring a successful visit for all.

On the Tour

Introduce the theme for your tour; firmly state the objectives for the tour and the desired learning goal. It may be tiring for babies and toddlers to stay with the group during the duration of the tour. Ask a parent or chaperone to help with the youngest children when needed.

If it is not possible or you do not choose to divide the group into age-specific activities, then look at the special challenges posed in accommodating a larger-than-expected variety of ages. Remember that in many cases the children are accustomed to learning together:

- *Where appropriate, use the team-teaching method*
- *Remember that storytelling and historical interpretation reach all ages.*
- *If you are alone, carry a basket of touchable objects appropriate for very young children as well as for older participants and rotate this experience during the time of the tour.*
- *Ask the older children to teach the younger children about the art or artifact in which they showed the most interest.*

Instead of insisting on your specific goal, try to involve the older children in the discovery tour for the younger children. At the same time, make appropriate information and vocabulary available to the older children.

Family Groups

Touring with family groups is an exciting opportunity for an intergenerational learning experience. The adults may have some museum experience, but can learn new skills to use with children during visits to other museums. They are usually enthusiastic about sharing a positive experience with the younger members of the group. Prior to the visit ask if they want a general museum tour, or are interested in specific areas or objects they want to see. Do they have specific goals for this museum experience?

Choose questions and activities to involve all members of the family group. You can encourage children to talk directly with an adult "buddy" about what each thinks/ sees/likes to promote a shared experience. Try to involve the youngest family members directly at some point, either with your question or a specific activity such as "can you find . . . ?" Younger visitors often have observations and questions that are quite unique, enriching the adult experience as well.

Note that the definition of "family" has changed in recent years and the children and adults in a group may not be related in traditional ways. Avoid such specific terms as parents, mom, dad, son or daughter. Use "grown-up" and "children" or "young people" to distinguish group members. Not everyone accompanying a child is a parent; adults may be step-parents, nannies, grandparents or other non-related adults. Not all children have a mom or dad with them and your group may be a "blended" family.

Lifelong Learning—An Ongoing Amazing Adventure

The commitment to lifelong learning for diverse audiences has challenged museums to create programs designed to connect larger numbers of visitors of every age group with objects and exhibits in meaningful ways. Museums want to make people feel that they are coming in as wanted and welcomed guests and not as trespassers into privileged territory.

Adult Audiences

Adults are in many ways the perfect audience for museum tours. They come to the museum not because they have to fulfill a learning requirement, but because they enjoy discovery, expanding their horizons and exploring new frontiers. They bring to the museum experience their own insights and knowledge and can contribute in exciting ways. Assess their interests and include information about the history of the region and the history of your institution. Avoid treating adult visitors like students. Use an engaging tone of voice and sophisticated vocabulary.

Touring with Older Adults

The needs of older adults can be met when you are prepared to go beyond your standard tour. A firm, gentle handshake and a warm smile immediately set the tone of your tour. Speak distinctly, not loudly, and face your audience. If possible, direct your visitors to a place where they may be seated for your introduction. Make your route clear to everyone and, in general, slow your

pace. Consider wearing clip-on microphones for voice amplification and carry large scale labels that all can read. Determine the length of your tour after evaluating the physical abilities of your group. Ask your group to let you know if they have any trouble hearing you.

An introduction that includes "remember when" or "compare and contrast" invites immediate participation and comfort. Docents in science museums can focus on technologies invented during the visitors' lifetimes. Art museum docents can build tours from paintings and sculptures of the mid-20th century. Opportunities are then provided for older adults to tell stories and share their own experiences. Allowing them to contribute benefits everyone. It engages the audience and can generate information that may be valuable in future tours. In history museums, audience members can add vital information to oral history. In any type of museum, encouraging visitors to talk about their experiences meets multi-cultural goals as well. Shared history is an effective way to create cultural links between people with diverse backgrounds.

Serving Visitors with Special Needs

The Americans with Disabilities Act (ADA) has placed a legal obligation on museums to make their buildings and services accessible to people with special needs. Aside from being mandatory, a willingness to be accessible and welcoming to all visitors can be an opportunity to attract new audiences of all ages and abilities. Each aspect of the museum experience should be considered in terms of accommodation of visitors with special needs. The way in which galleries are arranged and your attitude are important aspects for making visitors, whatever their status, feel comfortable and welcome.

Try to find out in advance which special needs your visitors might require. Familiarize yourself with how your museum accommodates visitors with special needs. Understand physical and mental impairment, blindness and deafness. You might want to get into a wheelchair and experience maneuvering it onto an elevator, into a restroom or in various galleries. What can you see and hear when sitting in a wheelchair? Accessibility for **chronically challenged older visitors** may require additional prior arrangements. If possible, prepare in advance to make available assistance devices such as stools, ramps, walking aids, assisted listening devices, or a docent microphone. [For helpful guidance

on disability etiquette, see for example, http://www
.unitedspinal.org/pdf/DisabilityEtiquette.pdf.]

Carefully choose exhibits that you want to introduce
to **visually impaired visitors**. Discover how a visually
impaired person experiences your museum. Where
permitted, handle an object with your eyes closed and
describe what you hold, as if you had never seen it. Ask
your museum to make available special museum gloves,
Braille labels and clear and effective signs. With proper
preparation, encourage visitors to touch with both hands
or guide their hands around an object. Use meaningful descriptive terms in describing objects; emphasize
texture and shape. [For help in crafting tours, see for
example, *Art Beyond Sight: A Resource Guide to Art, Creativity, and Visual Impairment* published by Art Education for the Blind and the American Foundation for the
Blind, http://www.artbeyondsight.org/sidebar
/aboutaeb.shtml.]

Hearing-impaired visitors appreciate a variety of
methods of interpretation to help them interact with
exhibits. Inquire whether the hearing-impaired visitor
will be accompanied by an interpreter. Make sure that
the interpreter has a clear idea of what you plan to
present and discuss. If time allows, make available a list
of objects and subject matters.

Face hearing-impaired persons and speak slowly so
that they can read your lips. Accommodate the interpreter for a deaf person and allow the interpreter to
become your shadow so that the visitor can observe
both of you at the same time and contribute to the tour.
In positioning yourself, make sure that light falls onto
your face.

In addition:

- *Stand at a comfortable distance.*
- *Ensure that your mouth is not obscured so that lip
  reading is possible.*
- *Speak clearly and without shouting.*
- *Speak neither too slowly nor too fast.*
- *Make one point at a time.*
- *Maintain eye contact.*
- *Use facial expressions.*
- *Use hand gestures.*

If hearing-impaired visitors are part of a larger audience that also includes hearing people, point out the
presence of hearing-impaired visitors and their interpreter. Ask hearing people not to obstruct the lines
of vision between audience and interpreter and to
keep as still as possible while you are talking. Provide
enough time for all participants to study the objects
and exhibits.

Assess the learning abilities of the **mentally challenged
visitors** and be prepared to meet behavioral challenges
such as interruptions, loud talking and napping. Care-
givers or aides can assist you in conducting a successful
tour. Ask another docent to team up with you for this
visit so that more than one pair of eyes and hands can
be used. Carry hands-on material and soft-textured
objects for those visitors who become easily distracted
and be prepared to move on at the first signs of rest-
lessness. Many museums are reaching out to visitors
with serious cognitive difficulties, including dementia.
[See for example, The MoMA Alzheimer's Project:
Making Art Accessible to People with Dementia,
https://www.moma.org/meetme/.]

Some helpful suggestions:

- *Limit tours to 4–6 persons plus a caregiver for each
  person with memory loss.*
- *Greet your guests at the door, expressing how pleased
  you are to see them.*
- *Introduce yourself and ask permission to use first
  names. Make name tags and put them on your guests.*
- *Keep the tour to 4–6 pieces of art. Limit your time to
  no more than one hour.*
- *Be conscious of your visitors' "eye level." Sit down if
  possible to increase communication.*
- *Ask each visitor specifically, not their companion, a
  question about what they see or feel. Their thoughts
  are often only in the moment. Do not use "remember
  when" phrases. It may cause anxiety because it may be
  difficult for these patrons to remember.*

Your positive attitude and a calm, reassuring manner
will allow your special needs tour participants to enjoy
their museum experience. And above all, be flexible.

6 On Seeing or Learning from Objects

We live in an age in which we are constantly inundated with images from newspapers, television and the Internet. Museums show us a dazzling variety of objects and images from every known culture and environment on Earth—and each of us approaches art, history, science and nature with different perspectives because of our unique personal histories and individual experiences.

You can look at objects in the museum as pieces of information the visitor can experience visually. Encourage them to observe and infer what they can from the objects themselves. During a museum visit, you want your tour participants to relax and enjoy a journey into seeing, exploring, focusing and learning by looking at art and artifacts. A successful experience will enable visitors to develop an appreciation for different styles, times and cultures. The following techniques might help you to accomplish this task.

Focus on the Object
The docent's first task is to focus a visitor's attention on the object. To achieve this goal, the docent should limit the number of objects to be seen. It is important for the docent to discriminate between information that is personally interesting and information that will be meaningful to the visitors. Objects can attract and hold visitors' attention while they stimulate curiosity and creative thinking. Before encouraging someone else to look at an object, it is necessary to really see it yourself. The information you choose should directly relate to the objectives of your tour. The following questions might help you get started:

- *Why have I chosen this object?*
- *What is its function?*
- *How does this object reinforce my theme?*

Accessing Information about an Object
Art and artifacts are basically composed of two- and three-dimensional facts. Docents can play a vital role in providing visitors with the keys to accessing information about these facts by presenting them in a manner to which the visitor can relate. Refrain from presenting too much information and from making an authoritarian impression. Give visitors the opportunity to look at the object in silence and allow them to visually explore the artwork, the object or the diorama.

Searching for Details
To focus visitors' attention, ask simple questions such as: "What do you see?" or "What is going on here?" You can enhance the discussion by asking the following questions that can relate to art, history, science and nature:

Medium:
- What does the artist/maker use?
- What do you think the object made from?

Color:
- What colors do you see?
- Why do you think they were chosen?

Texture:
- If you could touch it, what do you think it might feel like?

Shape:
- What organic or geometric shapes can you find?

Senses:
- What sounds do you hear when you look at this work?
- How is this like a piece of music?
- What smells do you associate with this type of setting?

With young students, you may want to try one of the following games:

The Whip—School children form a circle around an object. The docent goes around the circle several times, encouraging each child to produce a word that, in their opinion, describes the object. Speed is important. Soon the children will have discovered the obvious features and will begin to focus on more subtle details.

I Spy—Ask one student to find a detail in an object that might not be obvious to the other students, and to present clues about that detail using the phrase: "I spy something . . ." Additional clues may be presented until the object has been discovered.

Develop a Visual Memory

The best way to develop a visual memory is to encourage visitors to describe what they are seeing by using adjectives. Searching for words forces viewers to look for details in the object or diorama. By testing visitors' recall of objects you can help them to improve the clarity and the accuracy of their visual memory as well as hone their looking skills.

Shift Focus

Shifting focus will allow visitors to spend more time in front of a given object and discover features they might have otherwise overlooked. For instance, when looking at a bird, they might notice its colors first. Then, by shifting their focus to textures, they may become aware of the feathers on its wings or the scales on its feet.

The following two games can be used to emphasize the value of changing focus when looking. They can also introduce important elements to look for in paintings, plants or animals. For example, an arboretum docent might want to play the visual turn-around game with an emphasis on the colors, shape and texture of plants, while a history docent might want to highlight decorative motifs and functional elements.

Visual turn-around—Allow students one minute to absorb as much information as possible about a given object. Turn them away and ask, "How many figures did you find?" Give students the opportunity to check their answers by looking at the object. Repeat this exercise several times, instructing the students to focus on a different aspect of the object each time. During the first round, ask them to focus on color, during the second round on scale. During one of the following rounds let students select the items on which to focus.

Category games—Changing focus often entails altering the way people traditionally categorize items. Instead of looking at furniture in a period room, suggest that they look for objects that are the same color, made of the same material or have the same shapes.

Props for Focusing

Pencils and note pads may be useful, if allowed in the gallery. You may want visitors to sketch an entire object or to focus on specific aspects of an object. If your visitors are hesitant about their skills, stress that sketching is only a tool for looking and that their artistic skills are unimportant.

- *Magnifying glasses reveal details and intricacies barely visible to the naked eye.*
- *Mirrors held under or behind an object reveal different angles and perspectives.*
- *A Light Arrow Pointer or a strong flashlight will highlight details.*
- *Simple viewfinders such as cardboard rolls, holes in paper or cardboard or paper tubes narrow the field of vision and direct focus.*
- *Young children enjoy putting on "super-vision glasses" to explore an object.*
- *Tactile objects an be felt while exploring visual texture.*
- *Color chips can be compared to actual colors in artwork.*

The ideas discussed in this chapter center around seeing the object—an active seeing that challenges visitors to react to the museum exhibit. You as a docent are successful when you have enabled your visitors to voice their opinions, thus completing the cycle of exploration, discussion, learning and understanding.

7 Asking Questions: Observation-Based Touring

Whether you are a docent in an art museum or science museum, a botanical garden or historical site, conducting a successful tour is an art. It is not important how many objects visitors look at or how much information you provide—the importance lies in their developing observation, thinking and communication skills, and finding personally meaningful connections. In order to successfully guide visitors into developing these skills, you should master a series of questioning strategies that focus their attention on objects, involve them in creative and critical thinking, lead them to personal discoveries and challenge them to develop ideas and examine responses.

Why Ask Questions

In museums most objects are placed out of context. While some institutions have attempted to recreate the interior of a cathedral, the furnishings and decorations in a 19th-century East Coast Salon, sculpture gardens and natural environments, it is still difficult to come to a complete understanding of a specific object because museums cannot adequately recreate sound, smell, climates or a certain moment in history.

Observation and inquiry slow the pace, magnify what is seen and amplify what is felt, transforming visitors into learners. It is amazing what visitors can discover when guided by thoughtful questions. Different interests, experiences and backgrounds can contribute to a lively touring and learning experience.

Your questions have to fulfill several functions. They should:

- *initiate involvement and active participation,*
- *combine listening and speaking skills,*
- *shift attention from docent to object and set the agenda*

Types of Questions

The American Association for State and Local History identified four basic types of questions that encourage visitors to carefully observe and explore objects and to think about creative answers and opinions.

Cognitive/memory questions ask visitors to recognize or recall information. For example, questions such as: "When did the Civil War begin?" or "What was used to make this object?" are the narrowest type of questions, requiring a single answer that relies on memory and focuses on facts. This type of question is useful in assessing your group's background and in determining whether they have grasped information before moving on to a related point.

Convergent questions require explanations and encourage an explanation of relationships, comparisons and contrasts or problem solving. While several responses are possible, they tend to converge on one correct answer. The goal is to help visitors remember and organize questions. Convergent questions can ask visitors to translate information, e.g., "In your own words, explain how you would pan for gold" or "How do you think this pot was made?"

Divergent questions encourage visitors to explore several solutions to a problem by remembering information, organizing it and thinking creatively about it. Divergent questions have several correct answers. They ask visitors to apply what they know to a lifelike situation: "If you were in a rain forest, what would you do to survive?" or "If you were a bird, where would you build your nest in this garden?" Divergent questions can ask visitors to synthesize information by solving a problem in a creative way, e.g., "If this painting came to life, what would the figures do next?" or "What title would you give this work?"

Evaluative questions demand the formation and defense of an opinion. Visitors must organize information according to their own set of criteria, e.g., "Which object do you think best represents the Mayan culture and why?" or "Why do you think this object is on display?"

Asking questions that **you do not know the answer to** and genuinely want to know what others' answers would be can be a good overall strategy that leads visitors to participate and interact with each other.

Close-Ended Versus Open-Ended Questions

Close-ended questions encourage short and predictable answers. They are geared toward asking visitors to recall facts and give responses based upon prior knowledge. They can easily be answered with a simple "yes" or "no."

Open-ended questions challenge the visitor to observe and form an opinion. They encourage a variety of ideas, views and opinions.

Open-ended questions need careful planning and require purposeful sequencing. Always start with simple questions. People are very reluctant to make mistakes in front of their peers and need encouragement to respond to initial queries. As the group feels more comfortable, proceed with more challenging questions. The sequence of your questions is also critical when you help visitors discover concepts for themselves. Often more than one question is required and you must consider which questions need to build on previous answers.

Suggestions for Open-Ended Questions

At its most successful, this method demands answers that are subject to interpretation, discussion, explanation and evaluation.

Observation and interpretation

- *How would you describe this object (place, picture) to someone who has never seen it?*
- *How do you think this object was used?*
- *What is surprising or new to you? Why?*

Comparison

- *How are these objects (figures, animals, plants) alike?*
- *How are they different?*

Prediction

- *If you were in this diorama (painting, room), what problems might you face?*
- *What other . . . ? or How else . . . ?*

Facts

- *What is happening here?*
- *What do you see?*

Suggestions for Response Techniques

Facilitating group exploration demands responses that acknowledge each student's participation according to his or her own learning style.

Wait—Make available a reasonable amount of time for observation. Count to five before saying anything, indicating to your audience that you are expecting a thoughtful answer. If no one answers, try to clarify your question instead of answering it yourself. The five-second rule can also apply to students who have their hands raised before you finish your question. Explain that you are going to wait five seconds so that everyone has time to think. You will begin to see that responses are more detailed and that more students will volunteer to participate.

Listen—Focus on the person and maintain eye contact. Do not interrupt, even for clarification. Give nonverbal signs that show you are listening, such as concerned body posture, a smile or a nod.

Watch—Look for other students who want to respond or provide additional thoughts and recognize raised hands or eye contact.

Paraphrase—Repeat the response so that everyone can hear it. Emphasize visitors' comments to make it easier for all to remember what was said. Keep in mind that paraphrasing only changes the words and not the content. If answers do not seem to relate to your theme, encourage your visitors to present different points of view. Perhaps this is the time to add information in order to come to a satisfactory conclusion. If necessary, guide the discussion onto a new course.

Praise and reinforcement—Acknowledge the visitor's contribution, not the correctness of the answer. Open-ended questions have multiple answers appropriate to each learner's perspective. In contrast to "no" answers, responses such as "good" and "right" place value on the response and can stop active discussion by leading others to believe that they have nothing more to contribute. Try phrases such as: "You are helping us to think about this" or "Our understanding is growing."

Observation-Based Touring

Observation-based touring has been successfully employed in art, history and science museums. At the Tenth National Docent Symposium (Philadelphia, Pennsylvania, 1999) the Oakland Museum of California shared their techniques, reprinted by permission.

Art—Art carries multiple meanings, allowing group discussions to give rise to a number of reasonable points of view in a natural, unthreatening context. Participants can explore ideas freely in a group—in effect solving a complex problem cooperatively.

As they do this, several skills are developed that are transferable to all areas of cognitive growth and social interaction. Visitors are then able to establish a lively, thoughtful, personal relationship to art as they increase their competence in constructing meaning from a wide range of material.

- Pose the question: "What is going on in this painting (or artwork)?"
- Point out what the viewer says as he or she describes the artwork.
- Paraphrase what the viewer just said. Amend your paraphrase if necessary for clarity, making sure that the viewer agrees with it.
- Press for additional observations by asking, "What else?"
- Clarify a viewer's observation by asking, "What do you see in the artwork that makes you say that?" The viewer must give supporting visual evidence derived from the artwork to substantiate an interpretive observation.
- Build connections between differing opinions by saying, "One viewer sees this in the painting because . . . , and another viewer sees this because . . ." The opinions must always be supported by evidence from the artwork.

History—Objects help us document the history of people and their ancestors and the objects they have made and used in their everyday lives. Understanding what these artifacts reveal gives insight into the lives of people, what their possibilities and limits were, how they thought, what they valued and how they shaped their world. Using these objects as the starting point for observation-based questioning allows the docent to facilitate a discovery process that the visitor can then apply to other exhibits. Students have an opportunity to hone their historical thinking skills including observation-based interpretation, assessing historical evidence and connecting past, present and place. Observation, clarification and listening abilities are also developed.

- What is this exhibit about?
- Who lived here?
- What did the people in this display do?
- How are the objects different from what we have today?
- Why do you think this display is included in this gallery?

After each of the above questions, it is essential for the docent to ask, "What do you see to make you say that?"

- Point to the area the visitor is describing, allowing the group to focus on what is being said. Accept all answers as reasonable as long as they are grounded in the viewer's observations. Questionable responses will be sorted out by the group's interaction.
- Paraphrase what the visitors say. This gives validation to their comments and makes it easier for all to remember. It is important for the docent to wait a reasonable amount of time to allow visitors to fully observe the display, think about the questions and answer them.

Natural Science—Exhibits in natural science museums tell stories of plant and animal species in widely varying habitats. The exhibits emphasize the complex interactions of species within each environment. In natural science exhibits, there is often a right and wrong answer and a particular story played out. The docent's goal is to facilitate a discovery process through discussion without providing too much information. Docents engage visitors in discussions, encourage them to closely observe exhibits and then guide them in expanding their knowledge beyond what they have observed. The visitor develops a heightened awareness and appreciation for natural phenomena of the world outside the museum.

- What do you see here?
- What is going on here?

Accept all answers as reasonable. If the answers do not seem correct, encourage the group to give different points of view. Often the group will correct itself. Then, gently, provide accurate information, if needed.

- Point to what the visitor is observing.
- Paraphrase what the visitor says; clarify the observation. In viewing an exhibit of a coyote and wolverine confronting each other, the docent might say, "You observed that the coyote is like a dog. A coyote is related to dogs or the canine family. There are similarities."

- Clarify a viewer's observation by asking a variation of the question: "What do you see that . . . ?," for example, "What specifically do you see that shows you the coyote is like a dog?" Validating the visitor's comments makes it easier for the group to remember what was said and focuses the docent's attention on the visitors' experiences.
- Press for additional observations.

Use visitors' responses. Use their interest and observations to guide them in discovering a particular story. Provide some factual information when necessary to guide thinking and to create a successful learning experience.

When You Don't Know the Answer

When asked a question by a visitor, if you do not know the answer, admit it readily. It is not an embarrassment to admit that you do not know all the answers. Some visitors will find it a bit comforting to learn that a docent is not a walking encyclopedia. A challenging question can provide opportunities for extended contact with the group. Offer to do some research and mail the information to the class. Ask the questioner to do the research and contact you at the museum. Carry some self-addressed postcards for this purpose.

Benefits Gained from Open-Ended Questioning

Visitors will benefit from your tour if you guide them toward discovering rather than telling them what they are supposed to see and feel. They will become more responsive and enthusiastic and will have stepped out of the role of passive listener. Visitors will have learned to look, describe, analyze and respond—skills that will provide them with a foundation for future museum visits. Both personal and collective learning will be enhanced.

You will discover that no two tours will be alike and that your presentation does not become stale. Once you have mastered the skill of asking questions, you will feel an increased confidence in your ability to offer valuable tools to your audience. [For help with designing questions, see for example, http://museumtwo.blogspot .com/2009/04/ design-techniques-for-developing.html.]

YOUR PERSONAL NOTES

8 Act It Out! Hands On!

A wide range of movement and theater activities exist that involve visitors visually, physically, emotionally and intellectually with a painting, object or diorama.

Some activities encourage learning through nonverbal means and help visitors grasp concepts intuitively; others foster personal identification with people or events. Although movement and theater activities are often used with students, docents may be comfortable incorporating some of these activities into tours for adults. There are a variety of activities that can enhance tours for all ages.

Take a Pose
Posing can be used to illustrate differences between objects or living things.

For example, you might look at:

- *The difference between an animal poised for attack and one at rest or*
- *The difference between an Egyptian and Greek sculpture.*

Ask students to assume the two poses. By experiencing the different poses, visitors arrive at a better understanding of techniques and insights used in creating the two sculptures.

Move with a Purpose
Ask your visitors to move around while they are looking at objects. A simple action such as kneeling to observe a plant focuses the visitor's attention and makes the act of looking more memorable. When viewing a three-dimensional object, encourage the group to move up close and then back, to the side and down low, stressing the importance of different viewpoints.

Look with a Purpose
Asking the group to move about the gallery looking for specific objects of their choice changes the pace and gives visitors some browsing time with a purpose. Giving a prompt provides interest and direction. Which object would you most like to give your friend/mother/father? Which one says something about you? Which object makes you wonder about how it was made? Find as many examples of . . . as you can in this gallery. After choosing, visitors may want to share their choices and reasoning with each other.

Role-Play
Try character studies of people in portraits. If they came to life, how would they move? What might they say? Act out the proper way to enter and exit an Indian dwelling using a red yarn circle on the floor to indicate your dwelling stage. Perform a task by assuming the role of the animal shown in the diorama. How would an animal that has no thumbs pick up an apple?

Historical Interpretation
Bringing an object, a painting or a diorama to life through theatrics makes the subject more real. Re-enact a historic event or a daily routine from another century.

Props bring to life a static painting, sculpture or diorama. The prop can be as simple as a hat, an apron or a book. Your character becomes more and more impressive as it is explained through the words and mind of the character. Few docents have the time to make elaborate costumes, but any docent can apply this basic approach. For example, a female docent standing in front of a Remington painting or sculpture could speak from the perspective of a cavalry officer's wife or daughter. There are applications for costumed interpretation in all types of institutions. At natural science museums, the docent could become the famous historical figures John Muir or James Audubon or a contemporary naturalist or safari leader.

Storytelling

People of all ages love and remember stories. Stories establish connections not only between you and your audience, but also between the audience and the object. Storytelling docents are at an advantage because they have something tangible with which to start the story. Visitors are at an advantage when hearing a story in the museum setting—looking at the exhibit while listening to a story makes visualizing easier.

Preparation:

- Choose a short story that you like and read it aloud several times.
- Familiarize yourself with the story. Look at the page briefly. Look up from the page and visualize the scene. See, hear, feel, taste or smell what it is like to be there.
- Give each character a different voice and use each voice consistently throughout the story. Vary the pace. Learn to be comfortable with long pauses, using silence as effectively as you use words.
- Assume a different posture and/or facial expression for each character. Combine these gestures with each character's voice. Use your arms and hands to depict action or imagery.
- Practice telling your story in front of a mirror. Tape record or video record your story and listen to the recording. Look for ways to improve. Tell your story to a friend who will listen and provide constructive criticism.

Telling your story:

- Make sure your audience is physically comfortable.
- Be in the story with one part of your awareness. Use the script as a stimulus by taking some words from the script, and at the same time use words that evolve from the experience you are having with the story. Be with your audience with the other part of your awareness. Use their response as a gauge of their interest in characters or parts of the plot you may wish to embellish or abridge.
- Remember to vary your voice and body language.

Interaction after the story has been told:

- Continue to speak in the same animated fashion as when you were telling the story.
- Ask questions about characters in the story, such as: "How do you think he was feeling when that happened?"
- Shift gears to the present and discuss the lives of your audience.

- For example: "Some people feel that . . ." or "Do you know anyone who has had that experience?" Then follow with questions such as: "Have you ever felt like that?" Move from problems to solutions, encouraging your listeners to make suggestions to each other. Bring their awareness back to the present with questions that will elicit a response such as: "How do you feel about it now?"

Hands On!

Touchable objects on carts or presented by you on your tour offer a range of experiences that can enhance visitors' viewing and understanding of museum objects and specimens that are "do not touch." For visitors, there is a certain excitement about being able to look at every angle of an object, to weigh it in their hands or even to try it on. Suddenly more than one sense comes into play, or the original context for an object becomes clear and the objects behind the glass become much more real.

Hands-on material can be "real" examples or reproductions. They might be photographs to be passed around or shown on an iPad.

Working with hands-on material is exciting to audiences of all ages and is an excellent tool in working with children. It offers a concrete experience with an object, as opposed to more abstract words or concepts and can be especially helpful in explaining objects from more unfamiliar times and cultures. For the visually impaired, handling objects is a way of making collections more accessible. For any visitor incorporating senses other than seeing offers visitors a richer understanding of the objects in your collection.

For example:

- *Pass around samples of marble, aluminum and lead and allow the visitors to feel and weigh the specimens as they look at sculptures.*
- *Hand out bottles of spices to smell or taste when looking at cooking implements from different cultures.*
- *Investigate the differences between the man-made and machine-produced objects by examining glass from ancient and new civilizations.*
- *Pass around pieces of fabric such as lace or jewelry as pictured in a portrait.*
- *Feel the difference between meat-eating and plant-eating teeth.*
- *Offer firsthand experiences with tools such as wool carders, and drop spindles or wood-cut and etching*

printing plates, allowing visitors to discover for themselves the time and skill involved in their use.

- *Examine and feel the different size animal hair brushes used by artists.*
- *Use photographs and short video clips from iPads to illustrate techniques used in creating objects or provide brief historical context.*
- *Listen to a tape of music played on ancient musical instruments.*

Another use of hands-on objects is with a display cart and docent interpreter The cart and its objects often spark visitors' curiosity and eagerness to explore an exhibit in more depth. The cart allows you to supplement information provided by labels, and the close encounter with objects generates questions for you that might not arise during a tour.

Your objective in presenting hands-on material may vary, but should be connected clearly to the overall objectives of your tour. Include objects at the beginning of your tour to introduce concepts and generate interest. Link specific material to a selected object during your tour to enhance looking at details, deepen understanding of technique, use or context, and to generate questions and conversation.

In order to provide a successful experience in handling objects, it is necessary to give structure to this activity. Invite the group to form a circle or a double rainbow and be seated on the gallery floor. Of course, a group of adults can gather around your cart or basket in a circle as well. Demonstrate how to safely handle objects before distributing them. If possible, circulate more than one object at a time so that several visitors are involved at once. Be prepared for excitement and interaction among your visitors so that you know not to actively teach during the handling of the objects. Never rush through a hands-on activity as this may be the only time during the visit that your audience can thoroughly explore the REAL THING.

Gallery Activities

Consider other activities such as writing and sketching in the museum that can enhance engagement and enjoyment. Writing helps visitors think more deeply about the objects they are looking at, while sketching can promote closer looking at a painting, a sculpture, a beautiful flower or an insect.

Here are some ideas:

- *While looking at a landscape painting ask visitors to write a postcard they might send from that place describing the weather and surroundings.*
- *Use simple poetry in the form of a haiku or cinquain to have visitors describe feelings or thoughts in connection with an object.*
- *Sketch shapes, designs or even an entire object.*
- *Visitors can draw their own patterns for a rug or a personalized tea bowl.*

For children, assembling large floor puzzles of pieces in your collection, perhaps of a floor mosaic, a beaded bag, or a carved design on furniture helps them appreciate the intricate design or how it was made.

YOUR PERSONAL NOTES

9 Sensitive Issues

Museums increasingly look for new ways to attract larger and more diverse crowds to enjoy and learn from ever-changing exhibits. In addition to learning to satisfy the public's thirst for more knowledge and more exploration, you are challenged to handle a number of issues and questions with utmost subtlety and diplomacy.

Not all art and artifacts in museums are beautiful. Some exhibits focus on exploring the very essence of human creation, lay bare the human body, graphically show the ruthless destruction and extermination of peoples or offend religious groups. What is your obligation to the public when presenting controversial exhibits?

Ask yourself:

- *How do I feel about such exhibits?*
- *How can I objectively describe and discuss such an exhibit?*
- *What impact might my tour have on visitors?*

Nudity in Art

The issues of nudity and nakedness confront us constantly. It is impossible to ignore paintings and sculptures representing the bare human body. Therefore, prepare to deal with the subject of nudity in a professional and comfortable manner. If certain objects seem unsuitable for young museum visitors, or for you, avoid them on your tour.

Ask yourself:

- *Which approach is most comfortable for me?*
- *Which approach is most suitable for my audience?*

Very often you hear the question: "Why are there so many paintings and sculptures of naked people in the museum?" Adults might feel embarrassed or outraged. Young visitors will inevitably giggle and make remarks. The following suggestions will provide some ideas for a comfortable solution.

For very young visitors, cover your hand with a mitten and ask the youngsters to describe your hand. What are they able to learn about your hand once you remove the mitten?

Throughout time, artists, sculptors and craftsmen have depicted the human body in celebration of beliefs, philosophies, life and death. Artists are concerned with exploring truth and therefore show the body in its natural appearance.

- *In African art, the female body is a symbol of agrarian fertility.*
- *Sculptures from Melanesia depict nude males in celebration of fertility rites.*
- *In ancient Greece, a fascination with physical beauty and fitness evolved that has continued to influence artists throughout the history of Western civilization.*

Present the total picture:

- *Where did the artist stand in relation to the model when he carved this sculpture or painted this picture?*
- *How would clothing change our perception?*
- *How and why did the artist respect or exaggerate the rules of proportion?*
- *What do you think about the distribution of body weight?*
- *If you were the model, how long do you think you could hold that position?*

Explore nakedness versus nudity—the obscene and the aesthetically beautiful:

- *What does it mean "to be naked?"*
- *How does one feel in that condition?*
- *Would we feel differently when describing a "nude" body?*
- *What image does a "nude" body project?*

Exhibiting the Dead

For the last several hundred years, museums have exhibited a variety of preserved human bodies and skeletons. Many museums hold collections of remains of ancient peoples, mummies, body parts in formaldehyde and Native human remains and sacred and cultural objects. The media is filled with pictures of well-preserved human bodies found in bogs, in retreating ice fields or on remote mountaintops in the Andes that will sooner or later be sent on exhibition tours. These exhibits contain powerful pieces of information and should be treated with care and reverence. Inevitably they will evoke the following reactions:

- **religious**—such exhibits might violate laws of specific churches or cultures,
- **spiritual**—such exhibits violate the eternal rest and
- **aesthetic**—it is simply macabre or repelling to look at a dead person.

You may try to emphasize the unique quality of the specific exhibit and focus on scientific, biological, ethnological, cultural or historical questions that can lead to a discussion of:

- *What knowledge can we gain from such exhibits?*
- *How did certain societies treat their dead?*

Alternatively, you may choose to avoid the scientific justification and focus on the aesthetic value of such an exhibit:

- *When we look at a display of bones or skeletons— how do we feel when we realize that these are human remains?*
- *When we describe a collection of grave goods—aren't these items really funerary objects, selected for a specific deceased person to fulfill specific functions?*
- *When we describe excavation sites, burial grounds and certain archaeological digs—should we refer to them as sanctified grounds?*
- *What do you think it means to be the caretaker of human remains and sacred objects?*
- *What do you think it mean to treat these objects respectfully?*

Explore ancestor worship in other cultures and compare and contrast these rituals with those practiced by members of your group.

Assess your group's feelings before you embark on a discussion of how we think about our ancestors, and how we cope with death in our immediate environment.

A respectful and dignified approach can lead to a deep understanding of a controversial issue. You are challenged to see rituals through other people's eyes.

Religion / Religious and Sacred Objects

Museum audiences are composed of increasingly diverse religious backgrounds. Do not assume that each visitor has a broad knowledge of the many religions represented in American society today. When discussing objects that reflect various religions or belief systems, consider the following:

- Select a broad representation of religious objects.
- Provide information about the work's original context and meaning.
- Provide a narrative context for works of religious art.
- Prepare to tell the story of Osiris, Ganesha, Buddha or Jesus.
- Present stories with a sense of respect.
- Where appropriate, explain that some religious stories contain surprising elements in view of scientific truth and at the same time provide a feeling of comfort and special meaning to many people.
- Remain neutral and avoid showing your preference for a particular belief.
- Avoid the term idol and use the term religious sculpture.
- Talk about religious stories instead of myth.

Museums are challenged to find ways to present sacred art and artifacts in a secular culture without offending visitors. You might explain that:

- These objects were not meant originally to be seen within a museum setting.
- Each object would have been experienced within specific cultural contexts.
- Relics create intimate contact with a person. Skulls, certain bones, hair and other relics of important people in a religious or secular community or of family members were preserved and placed in special containers.
- In Western civilization, relics often connect to saints.

Depicting Suffering and Death

Throughout the history of art and sculpture, artists were concerned with realistically representing harsh and cruel times. Often viewers get the uncomfortable feeling that artists are recording rather than imagining the grueling scenes. Use these artworks for a discussion of significant historical events, for the exploration of spirituality and for a comparison of social conditions in the past and today:

- *What feelings do the scenes arouse in the observers?*
- *Did the artists accentuate certain details or did they create additional drama in order to arouse specific reactions?*

- *Did the artist work freely or was the artist in the service of the church, a monarch, or a dictator?*
- *Did the artist witness brutalities and suffering first hand?*
- *Did the artist suffer from poor health (e.g., mental illness, emotional problems) or live in poverty?*
- *In which social environment might the artist have lived?*
- *Which physical disabilities or restrictions placed upon them by society, gender discrimination or resistance to their ideas did artists have to overcome?*

Photography has opened an entirely new approach to the depiction of humanity.

Never before have we been able to so closely observe and partake in other people's lives, tragedies and suffering. The still and moving images are often shocking in their starkness. Therefore, the presentation of photographic exhibits requires intensive preparation and thoughtful insights into the subject matters. Social-historic facts and exhibits should be presented in such a way that visitors with no prior knowledge learn something and eventually are able to form their own opinions. Photos can be evidence. There may be no other style of presenting realities as graphic as photography. Keep in mind that those who are shown in the photo exhibits often did not give their consent.

Art and Artifacts of Indigenous Peoples

Your understanding of art and objects of the Ancient Americas, of Africa, Asia, Oceania, Australia, or Europe and the process in which they were created depends on your ability to place these images and items in context. Since not all cultures create "art for art's sake," some belongings that appear beautiful or artistic may have been created for utilitarian purposes. Here are some things to consider:

- *Why was the belonging created?*
- *What purpose does it serve?*
- *How was it created?*
- *What is the relationship between the maker and the user?*

It is helpful to develop an understanding of the historical changes in the social and geographical environments within which these objects and images were created. This will enable you to give meaning to a particular time in history, event, or to the life of a community leader or child.

Use proper language and terminology. Terms such as "primitive art," "tribal art," "ethnographic art," "folk art," and "non-Western art" were used in the past to describe the art of Indigenous peoples and ethnographic materials. These terms no longer should be used. Rather, identify the place of a belonging's origin as specifically as possible. For example, refer to a mask as Kwakwaka'wakw, rather than Pacific Northwest Coast. Keep up to date with changes in accepted terminology. Your museum's curators will be aware of this.

When introducing museum visitors to ethnographic material, take along a world map to point out the area that will be discussed. Explain geographic locations, climate, culture, history and the languages spoken.

Focus on a specific cultural group and consider the following questions:

- *Where do the people live?*
- *What climatic conditions can be found in the region?*
- *What materials were used to make this object?*
- *How did the creator use materials and tools?*
- *Do any of the forms, shapes, images and surfaces indicate anything to you about what this might be or how this object might have been used?*

When teaching visitors about how people live and work and what beliefs and ideals they cherish, give them the opportunity to make connections to their own cultural traditions, being mindful to not favor one culture over any other:

- *How would you describe this mask?*
- *How and when do you think it was used?*
- *Can you name occasions when you dress up?*
- *Which holidays in our society compare to ceremonies and holidays in the society we are discussing?*
- *What do you celebrate, what makes you proud?*
- *How do you celebrate coming of age?*
- *What makes a young man or woman in our society grown up?*

If you are comfortable, include in your discussion burial traditions and ancestor worship. Note that some communities consider these practices private and do not condone their sharing. Check with your museum's curator before proceeding.

- *Why were dishes, cups, storage vessels, miniature houses and replicas of villages put into graves?*
- *What can we learn through these objects about regional customs, lifestyles and beliefs?*

We all are intrigued by stories. Many belongings can be presented accompanied by stories to contextualize their places in the daily lives of the people who created, cherished, worshiped or used them. Be sure to verify a story's authenticity with people of the originating community and keep in mind that in some communities, stories are personal property. If you don't feel comfortable presenting objects through stories, consider having the visitors infer information regarding the belonging's creation and function.

Diversity

Since the second half of the 20th century, awareness, interest and pride have emerged in regard to our multi-cultural, multi-religious and multi-lingual society. Museums have become sources for sharing knowledge about the heritage and the many different peoples who once lived and who now live on the North American continent.

Museums must not only ensure that they are accessible to audiences of broader backgrounds; they must also develop a variety of cultural perspectives and acknowledge the presence of a multi-cultural society. Heritage events, festivals, music presentations and craft exhibits have become part of the museum scene. Printed multi-lingual guides to the galleries and foreign language tours are available in many museums.

Diversity topics and cross-cultural exhibits call for an interdisciplinary approach. Often such exhibits contain emotionally charged themes and issues. What you teach must take place within a broader vision. Careful planning is necessary, because during a timed tour you are able to present only a piece of the entire picture. Be prepared to accept a variety of responses and to deal dispassionately and objectively with difficult or controversial questions. The best way to avoid alienating visitors with traditional points of view is to involve them in the exploration of culturally diverse objects.

Various focal points could be:

- *the comparing and contrasting of American lifestyles, traditions and celebrations with those in other cultures,*
- *a discussion of environmental and ecological problems or*
- *a discussion of the roles and lifestyles of men and women of various colors, creeds and economic groups as you examine the art and belongings*

As an example, assume that you plan to explore a variety of objects from Africa such as masks and figures, jewelry, textiles and furniture and the roles they have traditionally played in people's lives.

Choose to discuss:

- *oral histories,*
- *colonization and modernization,*
- *changes or loss of traditions,*
- *independence from colonial rule and*
- *the value of new ideas and different viewpoints and how change is brought about*

Lead into a discussion of how a shared heritage can shape the artistic development of African-American artists, writers and poets. Diversity deals not only with differences among varied cultures and peoples, but also with issues of racism, poverty, history and religion. By sharing broad information about the past, you provide contrast to the present. Give enough information to allow for some connections to be made. Put information in a wide context to make it relevant to other groups and avoid introducing stereotypes related to ethnicity, race, sex or religion.

The more you know about others, the easier it will be for you to convey appreciation and sensitivity in concrete ways. Questions lead to discovery, investigation and a variety of responses. Be accepting of varied comments and responses and be prepared to overcome cultural barriers so that by your leadership you will be able to broaden your audiences' perceptions in a meaningful way.

The Dead Animal Issue—Is It Real?

The purpose of a natural history museum display is to stimulate interest in the natural world. Visitors will inevitably ask where the mammals, birds and reptiles on display come from and whether the museum killed them. A discussion of dead versus alive and real versus fake can be explored at every age level and should be introduced early in the gallery experience. Be prepared to respond to criticisms of those who believe that stuffed animals are degrading and ethically unacceptable and to talk about your museum's acquisition of the animals in the various exhibits. Specimens are material evidence and presented in the right context can be of great educational value:

- *They introduce city children to the rich life in natural environments.*
- *They raise awareness about biodiversity.*
- *They challenge visitors to think about the threat from humans and the chances for survival.*

You may want to explain how animals are collected today or discuss how a specific diorama is created introducing the concepts of taxidermy, habitat and endangered species.

A discussion of hunting trophies can lead to the discussion of hunts as a form of social activity, a sport, a means of gathering food and a means to control over-population in order to recreate balance in the environment and the food chain.

Evolution

In science, theory means "explanation"—scientific theories are not guesses or hunches as in the popular vernacular. They are more important than facts because theories make sense of observations (what we call facts). The Theory of Gravity explains why we don't float up to the ceiling. The Theory of Evolution is the scientific explanation of how life diversifies on this planet. When conditions on Earth change through temperature fluctuations, the formation of mountain ranges or rising and falling ocean levels, life on Earth changes. The process by which plants and animals adapt to these changes is known as evolution. When asked, "What is evolution?," the docent might reply:

- *"As far as we know in science today, evolution is . . ." or*
- *"According to this museum, the scientific explanation for the Theory of Evolution is . . ."*

The public's keen interest in fossils and dinosaurs and their questions based on that fascination can only be answered by an overview of evolutionary processes. However, when you face a group of school children, students or adult visitors you really have no knowledge about their religious beliefs and aesthetic values. You might enthusiastically present a program, especially in natural history and science, that turns out to be objectionable or offensive to some of your visitors or to some parents of school children. If your visitors appear to be receptive, you might try to explain the difference between religion and science by reminding them that religion answers the why questions of life and its ultimate meaning. Science answers the what, where, when and how questions in relation to what we can observe directly or indirectly from the natural world.

During the elementary grades, children learn biological concepts through direct experience with living things, their life cycles and their habitats. These experiences emerge from the sense of wonder and natural interests of children who ask questions such as:

- *Why are there so many different types of plants and animals?*
- *How many different animals are there?*
- *How do birds fly?*
- *Why do some animals eat other animals?*
- *Where did the dinosaurs go?*
- *How can certain plants grow in the desert?*
- *Why do children resemble their parents?*
- *How did things come to be that way?*

These questions will raise deeper questions, such as:

- *How old is the Earth?*
- *How old is the earliest human being?*
- *How do we know this?*

You are then challenged to lead a discussion of:

- *the diversity of life,*
- *interactions among all components of the natural environment,*
- *the certain order of organisms and*
- *balance in nature.*

Fossils are precious clues to the past. With the help of modern technology and exploration, scientists have been able to study the millions of species of plants and animals that live on Earth today and are related by descent from common ancestors. You may point out that consistent patterns of ancient to modern species found in the fossil record are strong evidence for evolution.

Many museums have displays to help visitors explore the fossil evidence of human evolution such as skulls, teeth, footprints and tools as well as animal and plant fossils. Time lines support visitors in exploring location and approximate age of these fossils.

Try some of the following activities in support of your tour:

- *Use modern anatomy as an effective technique. Encourage children to measure up to early humans in the exhibit.*
- *Examine the similarities of all boned animals in their basic limb patterns and explore their difference when adapting to changing environments.*
- *Examine the role of archaeological discoveries that lead to an understanding of extinct civilizations.*

Discussions can support your statements by examining the role of geologists, paleontologists and anthropologists in studying climate changes or life form changes found in the fossil record. Prepare for questions such as:

- *Do dioramas present the full picture?*
- *How do we know that the landscape was so barren at the specific point in the time line?*
- *How do we know that the sculptures of extinct humans actually resemble the people who lived so long ago?*

Sex and Reproduction

The topics of sex, coming of age, sexuality, sexual preferences and reproduction are being explored in museum settings as we become a more informed society. Yet taboos, reservations, embarrassment and even an "It doesn't exist" attitude remain in our diverse cultural and religious society. As confusion and conflicts have to be overcome, you are challenged to respond to the audience's curiosity with an open and comforting attitude.

No matter which collections and exhibits you present, whether they represent human behavior and attitudes and the artist's curiosity in Antiquity, the Renaissance, Baroque or the 20th century, whether they were collected at Indian temple grounds, in Japan, Africa or Oceania, you will encounter scenes referring to human sexuality and reproduction.

You can assume that many young visitors have been exposed to explicit television shows and have Internet access. To help lead a discussion involving sex or reproduction, try to familiarize yourself with:

- *your school district's curriculum guidelines concerning sex education,*
- *topics and issues appropriate for your group's age and*
- *scientific terminology for reproductive organs.*

A museum's main objective is to enable people to explore collections and exhibits for inspiration, learning and enjoyment. Sensitive issues are part of the experience.

As a docent, don't oversimplify presentations of sensitive issues, but rather show compassion and controlled emotions. Make sure that visitors can relate to the issues and build connections to everyday life.

As soon as you are able to successfully evaluate your own level of comfort and to master your knowledge about sensitive issues, you will be successful in supporting your institution's mission.

YOUR PERSONAL NOTES

10 Dealing with Problems

"We Want to See Everything"

Tour coordinators in your museum will hopefully point out that a tour can only cover selected areas or highlights of the collections. Teachers should be reminded that they should select objects in support of a certain curriculum topic or a discovery tour of a limited number of objects. When the group arrives, let them know what your plan for the tour is and reassure visitors that you have selected a representative number of objects or those objects that support their special interests.

If adults want to see more, invite them to explore the museum on their own and provide gallery information and floor plans.

Contemporary Art—"I Could Do That!"

Today's museums are places of experiences and happenings where the mind is as much engaged as the eye. Contemporary art may provoke reactions, discussions and even disbelief from visitors. Often visitors of all ages view contemporary art with a good portion of apprehension and feel that they have to share their points of view with the entire group. Use the excitement to your advantage and approach the problems with a spirit of adventure:

- *Instead of looking for any specific meaning in modern and contemporary art, focus on the energy that created those artworks.*
- *Pose challenging ideas: Just because the object looks easy to make, was it really easy to produce? How would you create an action painting?*
- *Focus visitors' attention on the techniques, materials and tools used to create the object and discuss characteristic elements of style*
- *Allow visitors to voice their likes and dislikes and guide them toward a discussion of contemporary art and artists' lives.*
- *Elaborate on certain historical and political events that made artists explore new directions.*

"This Is Boring"

As soon as you notice that your group's attention is lacking, e.g., rustling, whispering or glazed eyes, change the pace and focus of your tour, and give more choice and control to your group:

- *Involve visitors in question-and-answer exercises.*
- *Switch to a more interactive touring technique or tell a story.*
- *Change galleries or focus on the history of acquisitions in a particular gallery.*
- *Share the techniques of taxidermy and display.*
- *Use looking with a purpose so visitors choose what to focus on.*

If visitors imply that they have already seen this specific exhibit, you can either change galleries or invite visitors to share their observations from their first visit and whether they now view objects from a different perspective.

"Difficult" Kids

Young visitors often display a very short attention span and become restless and talkative or engage in interruptive and disturbing behavior. Prepare to be fully in charge throughout the tour:

- *Understand the various developmental stages of children and adolescents.*
- *Assess whether a certain behavior is part of the developmental stage or is unacceptable.*
- *Remember that inquiry touring techniques ask for involvement and that involvement creates excitement.*
- *Be aware of the fine line between excitement and unacceptable behavior.*

At the beginning of your tour, review appropriate behavior in the galleries and exhibits. Point out how close one can come to an object (preferably at arm's length). In some museums, one of the guards is designated to demonstrate and explain rules and proper behavior. Putting this responsibility into the hands of a guard frees the docent of authoritarian or disciplinary comments and sets a more relaxed tone for the tour.

It is unavoidable that problems arise with a restless group; therefore, consider the following ideas:

- *Spend less time in front of objects.*
- *Face the group.*
- *Call children's names frequently, but refrain from touching them.*
- *Acknowledge their participation.*
- *Alternate standing and sitting down in front of an object.*
- *Reinforce rules by complimenting good behavior.*
- *Introduce independent-looking activities.*

You may also try to ignore bad behavior. If that approach doesn't help, ask children to sit down in front of the object, take a deep breath and freeze for a moment. Ask them to close their eyes and imagine what it must feel like, smell like or taste like.

Encourage talkative troublemakers to share their ideas about certain objects:

- *"Let's relate your ideas to the work in front of us . . ."*
- *"I'd love to hear more about your ideas. Maybe we can discuss them further during browsing time or after the tour."*
- *"Thanks for your idea. Does anyone else have something to add?"*
- *"I'd like to bring you all back on focus . . ."*
- *"Let's explore a different object."*

Ask the group's chaperones to help If a group or an individual child becomes unruly, wanders off, or otherwise disrupts your tour presentation. If the group disturbs other visitors or endangers exhibits you have the option to cut the tour short and lead the group out of the gallery. Focus on a specific topic, regroup and, if time is left, continue the tour in another part of the museum.

"Difficult" Adults

It is important to maintain a courteous relationship with visitors, no matter how challenging it might be. Some adult visitors can pose problems that can steer a tour off course. When touring school groups, overly talkative teachers or chaperones can inhibit student participation. Acknowledge a teacher's (chaperone's, parent's) role in planning the tour and making the visit possible. It is important to preserve teachers'

dignity and relationships with their students and to keep communication with teachers open and pleasant. You can convey your expectations of the chaperones at the beginning of the tour as well, letting them know that you count on their assistance and support of the tour's progress.

Diplomatically mention at the outset that your tour was designed to meet the interests of a specific age category and that you are looking forward to the students' active participation in the tour. Tell students that it is their tour and that you are looking forward to their questions and comments. Keep eye contact with students only.

Call on students first. You might incorporate remarks by a persistent adult into your tour and compare their remarks to students' observations. Or when an adult asks a question you can pose the question to the students. If parents or chaperones stay in the background but continue to speak among themselves, ask them to come to opposite sides of the group to help move the group more efficiently, to pass out hands-on materials or to repeat the questions that you cannot hear. In doing so, be tactful, respectful and honor everyone's remarks.

Adult visitors sometimes have a lot of knowledge of the subject or object you are discussing and want to share their comments with the group. You may also have adult visitors that believe they are highly knowledgeable about the subject under discussion but may be misinformed or have old information that is no longer valid. It is easy to lose control of the tour if such a person is persistent, talks too much and dominates the conversation. You can acknowledge their familiarity with the subject, and give them some time to offer their contributions. However, you want to make it clear that everyone in the group needs time to share observations and ideas.

At times, visitors may challenge your information, based on their knowledge or personal experience. Again, politely acknowledging their view, while presenting what you have understood to be factual based on the museum's and curator's work, is the respectful approach. Of course, if you have reason to think you may be incorrect or inaccurate, acknowledge that fact as well.

11 Looking Back & Facing the Future

The last five minutes of a tour can be as critical as the first five minutes. All too often, time runs out before a proper conclusion can be made. It is important for you and the visitor that you take time to tie up loose ends.

Review What Visitors Have Seen or Done
A quick review at the end can reinforce the major points of your tour and give you an indication of what your group learned. Try to make the review fun and not like a test at school:

- *Ask your group what they liked best. If they were allowed to take one object home, what would they choose and why?*
- *With younger visitors, this can be posed as a question of liking or disliking; older groups can think about the significance or representation of an object.*
- *Ask them what they remember most.*

Encourage Visitors to Return
Pass by the entrances to other galleries on your way to the exit or mention something spectacular you weren't able to show. Invite visitors to return with their families and friends and encourage them to be the docent for their own groups. Give a brief overview of coming attractions or new installations.

Leave your group with something that will remind them of their visit and encourage them to return. For adults, this could be a quote or provocative question. For students, it might be a sticker, a postcard or an activity for the bus ride or classroom.

Some Questions to Consider
After the group leaves the museum, it is time to reflect. Sometimes, new insights are gained from successes and other times from failures. So that your tour is a continual learning experience, try to evaluate your performance using the following questions:

During my tour did I:
- *set the stage for an effective tour?*
- *arrive in time to receive pre-tour instruction?*
- *check with the teacher to find out what is expected?*
- *get acquainted with the group (introductions, reinforcement, etc.)?*

Share the five "Ws"?
- *Who I am.*
- *What I am.*
- *Where we are.*
- *What we will see and do.*
- *When we will be finished.*

Provide information in an interesting way?
- *Offer a theme, major concepts and summary.*
- *Pick up a theme initiated by my audience.*
- *Be factually well prepared, adding new information regularly.*
- *Avoid trying to tell all I know about the gallery.*
- *Employ appropriate vocabulary.*
- *Use role-playing, storytelling and cart materials.*
- *Direct browsing time using assignments, treasure hunts, etc.*

Use successful touring techniques?
- *Appear confident and friendly.*
- *Make sure my voice carries to the back row.*
- *Display enthusiasm about my subject.*
- *Make eye contact.*
- *Wait until everyone is listening before I begin.*
- *Avoid distracting mannerisms like key rattling or pacing.*
- *Make plans for smooth transitions.*
- *Use positive reinforcements to encourage group participation.*
- *Know an alternative plan for unruly groups.*

Complete the tour?
- *Lead my class out of the museum on time.*
- *Encourage repeat visits.*
- *Thank the group for their interest and participation.*

Critically review my presentation and plan to improve by:

- *additional study,*
- *monitoring a fellow docent's performance and*
- *practicing with another docent.*

Your responsibility as a docent is much more than a curriculum extender, a free day guide or a substitute for the teacher. You are the public face of your institution and have the special opportunity to share not only your knowledge but also your enthusiasm for opening the world of art, history, science and nature. A tour can be more than a single event in a person's life. Teach your visitors how to learn by looking.

Enable them to discover more on their own and become lifelong museum enthusiasts.

Technology and the Docent

Technology is revolutionizing our world and the way people interact with each other, the museum, and with you as a docent. Museum leaders are struggling with how to thoughtfully integrate technology to enhance the visitor experience while maintaining personalized encounters with objects and spaces, as well as opportunities for reflection and quiet discovery. You confront the challenge of a rapidly evolving and constantly changing technological landscape. We live in a digitized world where the use of technology is a part of our lives. Electronic devices of all kinds are in use everywhere and museums are no exception. But keep in mind that despite our virtual/digital world, visitors still love encountering the real thing.

Television monitors, video screens, and tablets have become integral parts of many exhibits: interviews with curators and artists shown on monitors can enhance exhibits—delivering background information or demonstrating artistic techniques such as etching or block printing. Because children love to watch videos it is easy to lose their attention; adults, too, may wander away to watch monitors.

Interactive tablets are often available for a "hands on" experience for visitors. Cell phones and cameras add another layer of confusion. In addition, visitors may be using provided electronic tours and cluster at objects where you also want to stop on your tour.

For docents the use of electronic devices can pose a challenge, making navigation through galleries difficult; while delivering informative and interesting material, they can also be a distraction. As in all tours, flexibility is important!

Here are some suggestions and strategies for touring and the most commonly used technology.

TV Monitors and Videos

If monitors and video screens are in use with exhibits in the museum

- *Ask if the volume can be turned down while your group is there.*
- *Depending on the length of the presentation, plan to use the information as part of your tour, remembering that you may not know what part of the production you will encounter.*
- *Try to avoid monitors and larger screens if you find them intrusive; if that is not possible, have your group watch for a few minutes and work the information into a discussion.*

Tablets

Your museum may provide interactive tablets for some exhibits. If so, briefly explain or demonstrate their use if you plan to include this activity in your tour. You may want to use your own tablet with images to use.

For example

- *If looking at an artwork of a particular place, find an image of the same place by another artist.*
- *In looking at Inuit art, show photos of how indigenous people adapted to harsh winters—their clothing, housing, how they hunt and fish.*
- *While looking at ancient tools, show photos of how tools have changed and developed over many years.*
- *While discussing migration of animals, use photos and graphs showing migration patterns.*

Smartphones

Visitors, whether adults or students, increasingly use their smart phones to photograph and do on-the-spot "research." Museums' policies with respect to photographing are evolving and you will need to be clear about what is allowed in your museum. When touring with school groups clarify with the teacher what is expected/allowed on the museum visit. Often visitors want to photograph while touring. It can be helpful to explain to the group that you will pause several minutes before moving on to the next stop to give the group an opportunity to take pictures.

Some exhibits include labels that encourage the use of phones to learn more about an object. For a school tour, plan ahead with the teacher to decide if it would be useful to incorporate the use of smart phones into your tour.

Because time is limited in a tour, you may choose not to make use of electronic devices in the museum. Explain to visitors that monitors, tablets and electronic tours provide supplemental information that can enhance the exhibits; invite visitors back to take advantage of digital information, learn more about a particular exhibit or explore other parts of the museum.

Here are some facets of technology used by docents or in collaboration with docents—all with the ultimate goal of improving the visitor experience, offering alternatives and appealing to new audiences:

- *Docent websites for communication and education*
- *Digitally recorded art history lectures to be posted online for docent reference and further education*
- *Electronic newsletters among docents*
- *Online tour count reporting*
- *An iPad image database to aid in touring or short video clips to provide context or illustrate technology*
- *Social media for invitations to tours and blogging on art or other topics (usually done in collaboration with the docent's institution)*
- *Headsets for large tour group*
- *Games and gamification incorporated into tours*

Evolving use of technology is a dynamic topic and continually needs to be revisited and updated. The best place to look for the latest docent practices is on the National Docent Symposium Council website www.nationaldocents.org. Posted in the Symposia Section/Breakout Sessions/Technology, look for sessions previously presented at the past symposia that highlight technology. Perhaps your docent group has successfully incorporated some facet of technology related to being a docent—if the answer is yes, consider presenting your success story in a breakout session at the next symposium!

YOUR PERSONAL NOTES

History of the National Docent Symposium

Recognizing the desire to organize a forum for the exchange of ideas among docents, guides and interpreters, the docents at the Indianapolis Museum of Art organized the first nation-wide meeting in 1981. In the course of the following four years a steering committee agreed to organize biennial symposia for docents from all museum disciplines and the concept of a National Docent Symposium Council (NDSC) was formalized. In 1988 the National Docent Symposium Council was incorporated as a nonprofit organization under the laws of the State of California and federal tax exempt status was obtained. The Council Board of Directors is composed of two directors for each of six regions designated regions in the United States and Canada. The symposia are organized by volunteer docents and guides, for volunteer docents and guides, and offer a wide variety of workshops, lectures and round table discussions as well as opportunities for visiting on-site museums, historic homes and botanical gardens.

A kaleidoscope was chosen as the symbol for the 1987 National Docent Symposium sponsored by the docents of the Toledo Museum of Art. It was consequently adopted as the logo for the National Docent Symposium Council.

The following National Docent Symposia have taken place or will be held at the invitation of the docents and guides of the host institutions:

1981   Indianapolis Museum of Art, Indianapolis, Indiana

1983   Milwaukee Art Museum, Milwaukee, Wisconsin

1985   Oakland Museum of California, Oakland, California

1987   Toledo Museum of Art, Toledo, Ohio

1989   National Gallery of Art, Washington, DC

1991   Denver Art Museum, Denver, Colorado

1993   High Museum of Atlanta, Atlanta, Georgia

1995   Natural History Museum of Los Angeles County, Los Angeles, California

1997   Seattle Art Museum, Seattle, Washington

1999   Philadelphia Museum of Art, Philadelphia, Pennsylvania

2001   The Marion Koogler McNay Art Museum, San Antonio, Texas

2003   The Art Institute of Chicago, Chicago, Illinois

2005   Fine Arts Museum, Boston, Massachusetts

2007   Phoenix Art Museum, Phoenix, Arizona

2009   Art Gallery of Ontario, Toronto, Ontario

2011   St. Louis Art Museum, St. Louis, Missouri

2013   Fine Arts Museums, San Francisco, California

2015   Museums of Cincinnati, Cincinnati, Ohio

2017   Montreal Museum of Fine Arts, Montreal, Canada

2019   Smithsonian Freer | Sackler Gallery, Washington, DC

2021   Nelson-Atkins Museum of Art, Kansas City, Missouri

2023   High Museum of Art, Atlanta, GA

Suggestions for Additional Reading

A large number of books inspire us in many different ways, and each one of us has favorites from which we draw knowledge. The list of books we provide here is meant to merely start a list of reference works that provide additional information.

- Berger, John. (2008). *Ways of Seeing*. Penguin Modern Classics.
- Burnham, Rika and Elliott Kai-Kee. (2011). *Teaching in the Art Museum: Interpretation as Experience*. Getty Museum.
- Gardner, Howard. (1982). *Art, Mind, and Brain: A Cognitive Approach to Creativity*. New York, NY: Basic Books.
- Gardner, Howard. (1983). *Frames of Mind*. New York, NY: Basic Books.
- Gardner, Howard. (1991). *The Unschooled Mind: How Children Think and How Schools Should Teach*. New York, NY: Basic Books.
- Gartenhaus, Alan. (1997). *Minds in Motion: Using Museums to Expand Creative Thinking*. Third edition. San Francisco, CA: Caddo Gap Press.
- Gordon, Lawrence and Sommer, Eleanor. (2009). *People, Types, and Tiger Stripes*. Fourth edition. Gainesville, FL: Center for Applications of Psychological Types.
- Grinder, Alison L., and E. Sue McCoy. (1985). *The Good Guide: A Sourcebook for Interpreters, Docents and Tour Guides*. Scottsdale, AZ: Ironwood Publishing.
- Hayes, Jennifer Fell, and Dorothy Napp Schindel. (1994). *Pioneer Journeys: Drama in Museum Education*. Charlottesville, VA: New Plays Books.
- Hein, George E. (1998). *Learning in the Museum*. New York, NY: Routledge.
- Hughes, Catherine. (1998). *Museum Theatre: Communicating with Visitors through Drama*. Portsmouth, NH: Heinemann.

- Melton, Arthur W., Nita Goldberg Feldman, and Charles W. Mason. (1996). *Measuring Museum Based Learning: Experimental Studies of the Education of Children in a Museum of Science*. Washington, DC: American Association of Museums.
- National Aeronautics and Space Administration. (1994). *Discovery for Children in Grade K–3/National Air and Space Museum, Smithsonian Institution, in Collaboration with National Aeronautics and Space Administration*. Washington, DC: National Aeronautics and Space Administration, Office of Human Resources and Education, Education Division.
- Pond, Kathleen Lingle. (1993). *The Professional Guide: Dynamics of Tour Guiding*. New York, NY: Van Nostrand Reinhold.
- Thompson, Christine Marme, ed. (1995). *The Visual Arts and Early Childhood Learning*. Reston, VA: National Art Education Association.
- Torrance, E. Paul. (1976). *Guiding Creative Talent*. Huntington, NY: Robert E. Krieger Publishing Company.
- Yenawine, Phillip. (2013). *Visual Teaching Strategies: Using Art to Deepen Learning Across School Disciplines*. Harvard Education Press.
- Zelanski, Paul, and Mary Pat Fisher. (1999). *The Art of Seeing*. Fourth edition. Upper Saddle River, NJ: Prentice Hall, Inc.

Ordering Information

Sponsored by the National Docent Symposium Council

Please visit our website for current pricing
and order information.

www.nationaldocents.org

CPSIA information can be obtained
at www.ICGtesting.com
Printed in the USA
BVHW021435060321
601619BV00003B/87